LIFE ON
GOD'S ISLAND

From the same author

Life with the Coal Tar

Stories from Campbeltown's
West Coast fisherfolk

From book and craft shops or s.a.e. to:
PO Box 3 Ellon AB41 9EA

ISBN: 0-905489-58-6

Northern Books from Famedram Ellon AB41 9EA www. northernbooks.co.uk
Printed in Scotland

Life on God's Island

STORIES FROM
THE INNER HEBRIDEAN
ISLE OF GIGHA

FREDDY GILLIES
Photographs Sandra Howden

Northern Books
from Famedram

Contents

V. T.   DOLPHINS

Introduction

To say that I saw the Island of Gigha for the first time on an inky black night in February 1973 is not entirely accurate. True, I was serving as a deckhand aboard the Carradale prawn trawler 'Bonnie Lass' (CN 115), skippered by my uncle Ronnie Brownie, and we had just tied up at the island's South Pier following a traumatic half-hour trying to find the unlit jetty through a narrow rock-strewn channel. But I felt Gigha, rather than saw it. I was aware of shadowy figures, barely illuminated in the minimal glow cast by the boat's deck lights, moving around on the pier above and the permeation of the foc'sle stove smoke hanging in the still, frosty night air added to the general eeriness of the scene.

The fact that we had just begun prawn fishing and were, consequently, unaccustomed to dealing with any form of bulk, meant hours of painstakingly sorting the catch and a late dinner before gratefully rolling into our bunks.

I was disappointed. A curious desire to see the islands of Scotland had been growing inside me for some time. Perhaps it had something to do with my St Kildan ancestry, or maybe it was because, at that time, I had developed an appetite for any literature that dealt, however remotely, with the offlying jewels of Scotland's west coast.

But I was not to be despondent for long. Two days later, thanks to the vagarious nature of the Scottish weather, a north-westerly gale put paid to any hope of fishing and I spent a glorious day, albeit a chilly one, wandering around until fatigue and hunger got the better of me.

Something struck a chord then and forged a fondness for Gigha and its people which has never left me.

Twenty-three years later, by some incredibly fortuitous stroke of luck I was given the opportunity of joining the crew of the Caledonian MacBrayne car ferry which serves Gigha and I now find myself living and working on this lovely isle.

Back then in 1973 and the years immediately following I got to know just about everyone on the island, whether it be over a wayside chat or a generous drink in the hotel. With the passage of time a lot of these friends are gone but their memories fill me not with grief; more with the satisfaction of having known them.

The first two men I met on Gigha are, fortunately, very much alive and kicking. Calum McNeill and Neil Bannatyne were on the pier the night I got my feet on to Gigha for the first time and are still kenspeckle figures on the island today.

Probably my favourite port of call was at Gigalum Cottage, home of Angus and Charlotte MacAlister, along with their two sons, John and Archie. John, a scallop fisherman of national renown, has recently taken delivery of a new £1m purpose-built clam dredger and no longer lives on Gigha but brother Archie still fishes from the island. Charlotte passed on a few years ago but Angus, now aged 81 and despite having had major heart surgery, is as active as he was when I first knew him.

It is difficult to describe in words the welcome which invariably awaited at Gigalum Cottage but one can sense when something is truly genuine. Angus was forever pressing hospitality, be it food or drink, upon me and I remember one stormbound day I looked in around lunchtime.

"Now, ye'll jeest stay for yer dinner," he instructed me. My protestations that a meal would be served soon on board the boat was met with the reply: "It's a bad job if a young fella' laik you canna eat two dinners." And two 'dinners' I did eat!

As the nights drew in Angus would produce his button accordion and entertain us with an impromptu selection of his favourite tunes which always seemed to sound better if there was a wee dram on the go. How he picked out the melodies with his big fingers, calloused by years of fencing and hand-hauling lobster creels, always intrigued me.

Another great friend of mine was James McNeill, better known to all as 'Jimmocks', who returned to his native Gigha after spending a long time working as a lorry driver on the mainland. Jimmocks was the island's unofficial entertainments officer and he revelled in organising dances and discos, never being downhearted by the fact that sometimes attendances left much to be desired. I was a guest on many occasions for a meal with him and his elderly mother in the trim shoreside cottage called Tigh Na Rudha, and many a ploy we were involved in.

Sadly, Jimmocks left us in the mid-eighties but I am sure he was looking down and laughing at me on the evening of his funeral. I crossed to Gigha to attend the service and, as so often happens on such occasions, had drunk far more whisky than was good for me. I had arranged to stay with Jimmocks's brother, Alasdair – coincidentally in the house in which we now live – and was making my way there in a shambling manner in the pitch darkness when, I suppose inevitably, I fell into a roadside ditch. My light grey 'pure new wool' three-piece suit was in almost as sorry a state as its owner and I was grateful when Alasdair gave me a change of clothes.

However, I did not entirely appreciate his subsequent actions when he stuffed my suit into his wife's automatic washing machine, followed by a session in the tumble dryer. To the extreme merriment of the ferry crew, I made the crossing to Tayinloan the following morning nursing a fearful hangover and dressed in a suit that might have fitted a 12-year-old at a push! It is impossible when writing about friends to name everyone and, short of tabulating a highly impersonal list of names, it is not practical here but I am sure all my friends on Gigha know I am thinking of them.

Gigha truly is a haven of peace and tranquillity where one can almost hear the silence at times. Although there are obvious inconveniences not readily identifiable on the mainland the quality of life on this crime-free island is second to none and I, for one, am pleased to be part of it.

A few Gigha names...

GIGHA	
(1) Norse Gja-ey	*Creek, or Rift Is.*
(2) Gaelic Eilean Dhia	*God's Island*
(3) Norse Gud-ey	*God's Island*
PORT NA GALLOCHILLE	*Gallochille Bay,*
ARDMINISH	*Middle Ness*
ACHAMORE	*Big field*
CAIRNVICKOYE	*MacKay's Cairn*
KEILL	*The Cell*
TIGH CREAGACH	*Rock House*
DRUMACHRO	*Ridge of the fold*
CREAG BHAN	*White rock*
ACHAVENISH	*Field of the narr*
DRUMEONMORE	*John's big ridge*
DRUMEONBEG	*John's small rid*
PORT RIGH	*King's bay*
KINERERACH	*East Head*
ACHNAHA	*Field of the kiln*
ARDACHY	*High field*
SGEIR-NA-HATHA	*Kiln Rock*
SGEIR-NAN-RON	*Seal Rock*
TIGH NA RUDHA	*Point House*
TAR AN TARB	*Loch of the Wate*
PORT NAN CUIDAINNEAN	*Bay of the cuddies*
GARBACHA	*Rough field*
DUN TRINSSE	*Trench fort*
ARIDANLEIM	*Sheiling of the Spouting*
BAGH	*A bay*
RUDH	*A point*
BELMOIR	*A big homestead*

The Island

Historians argue whether the Island of Gigha was named 'Gud-ey', meaning God's Island, or 'Gja-ey', describing an island of creeks, by the Norwegian King Hakon when he arrived there in 1263 with more than 100 boats to prepare for his conflict with King Alexander III of Scotland at the Battle of Largs.

Personally, I will settle for God's Island – a sentiment which I am reasonably sure is echoed by anyone who has ever had the good fortune to visit Gigha.

This little gem of an island, a mere six miles long and barely two at its greatest breadth, narrows to only 400 yards at the Tarbert isthmus. It lies three miles off the Kintyre coast, directly opposite the hamlet of Tayinloan, and is reached by crossing the Sound of Gigha.

Gigha is still unknown to a surprising number of mainland Scots and many people struggle with the pronunciation of its name. It is best to disregard the 'gh' and say it as 'Gee-ahh' with a hard 'G'.

The island has a shoreline which can probably be best described as being irregular, with many gullies, black rocky inlets and incredibly white sandy bays which stretch the coastline to almost 30 miles.

The waters which wash gently ashore when Mother Nature is in placid mood have a clarity which really has to be seen to be believed. On one of those unforgettable endless summer days, when the sun throws its warming rays upon a windless Scottish west coast, Gigha rises like an emerald from a tranquil sea which ranges in colour from turquoise through aquamarine and azure to deep sapphire, unrivalled even by the Caribbean.

And yet in winter, when the Atlantic is angry and surging

breakers roll relentlessly under scudding grey storm clouds to vent their fury on the western shore of the island, there is still something bewitching about it all. The sinister, black jagged fingers of the Gigha Sound's semi-submerged reefs stand in defiance of the mighty sea, and sheets of spray high in the air bear testimony to the rocks' perpetual resistance to such unbridled power.

Gigha is a green and fertile place with many acres of lush pasture subdivided into several farms which support prime dairy herds.

Parts of the island are heavily wooded and there are several lochans dotted here and there. Wonderful views can be had from the top of Creag Bhan, Gigha's highest peak at 331 feet. From this vantage point, Islay, the Paps of Jura, Scarba, Ben More on Mull, Knapdale, the Mull of Kintyre, Rathlin Island, and the coasts of Northern Ireland and Donegal can all be taken in. On a crisp autumn morning, the colours witnessed in this panorama are captivating and it would take tremendous artistic talent to capture the scene on canvas.

Gigha's diverse habitat attracts many birds, both breeding and migratory and more than 120 different species have been recorded. Occasional sightings of some of the rarer breeds include the Great Skua, Pintail, Leach's Petrel, Icelandic Gull and Egret.

Scandinavian visitors include Brambling, Fieldfare and Redwing and a few of the birds which have nested in the gardens of Achamore House are Goldcrest, Sparrow Hawk, Dunnock, Siskin and Pied Wagtail.

Residents of the rougher heathland around the island include Curlew, Redpoll, Blackcap, Spotted Flycatcher, Wheatear, Whitethroat, Sand Martin and Lapwing.

Seabirds, naturally, abound. The duck population is well represented by Eider, Mallard and Shelduck and other species such as Black Guillemot, Red Breasted Merganser, Rock Pipit, Redshank, Arctic Tern, Mute Swan and Heron can all be seen along with the more common Gull, Fulmar and Gannet.

Breeding predators on Gigha include Buzzard, Barn Owl, Hen Harrier, Kestrel, Merlin, Peregrine, Sparrow Hawk and Raven.

The island is liberally carpeted with wild flowers of all descriptions. Spring sees the appearance of Celandine, Primrose, Purple Violet, Bluebell, Iris and Marsh Marigold. Summer blooms include Foxglove, Dogrose, Burnet Rose, Red Campion, Lousewort, Water Aven and Marsh Cinquefoil. In particular abundance is the Common Spotted Orchid and, to a lesser extent, Broad Leaved Marsh Orchid and Fragrant Orchid. These are but a few examples of the 120 different types of wild flowers which have been catalogued on Gigha.

Common seals frequent the rocky coastline and do not seem to have any territorial preference, being found in equal numbers on both the east and west shores. The otter is more secretive, but it is fairly easy to observe him at play in the many tiny bays and rocky ports.

Few people, even on Gigha, can have had the opportunity of viewing an otter at such close quarters – though perhaps not through choice – as Miss Fiona Henderson, who lives in one of the Ardminish village houses.

On a dark night during October, 1997, Fiona opened the back door of her home to go outside for some coal and was vaguely aware of an animal-like shape darting past. On re-entering the house she was astonished to find a fully-grown otter in the living room. The creature appeared to be in some distress and knocked over a table lamp and other pieces of light furniture before making good its escape via the kitchen. Fiona thinks she saw traces of blood on the otter and reckons it could have sustained its injury in a fight with another animal.

Porpoises have been regular visitors to the Gigha Sound for many years and take great delight in swimming along with the ferry or the fishing boats.

Dolphins have now appeared in the area and a school of twelve was noted on an afternoon of late summer warmth and calm in September, 1997. Many visitors to the island have been fortunate in photographing the dolphins from the upper decks of the ferry during the short sea journey across the Sound of Gigha.

Gigha is, I suppose fortunately, bereft of the more destructive form of wildlife. There are no foxes, stoats, wildcats, weasels, badgers or hares, but the mice and rat population is reasonably healthy! There are also a few feral cats, the domestic cat which has been left to roam at will.

The unpolluted waters surrounding the island support many sea creatures, including crabs of all kinds, limpets, periwinkles, sea urchins, starfish, 'buckie' whelks, lobsters, crayfish, prawns, scallops and sandeels. In addition, good stocks of lythe (pollack) and saithe (coal fish) can be found close inshore on the west side. Shoals of mackerel usually make an appearance during the summer months and provide, with the lythe and saithe, good sports fishing.

Indeed, my friend William Howden and I between us took an impressive 64 big lythe and 140 mackerel during a five hour fishing trip in August, 1996.

Although Gaelic-speaking is making something of a comeback on other Scots islands this, unfortunately, is not the case on Gigha. In living memory there were very many Gaelic speakers but nowadays there are less than ten people on the island who can converse fluently in the 'old tongue'.

Gigha's main housing settlement is at Ardminish, in the southern part of the island on the east side, and consists of some 15 dwellings with a further four at nearby Burnside and four at Woodside.

The Gigha Hotel is but a few minutes walk northwards from Ardminish and a cluster of buildings a little further on form the 'administrative centre'. Here is found the Post Office and shop, Gigha Primary School and schoolhouse and the island's Presbyterian church. In addition, there are both residential and holiday homes and the church manse in the immediate vicinity.

Unfortunately, Gigha's principal export continues to be people and the population at the time of writing, in 1999, stands at 120. The population peaked at 614 in 1791 and was still a healthy 401 in 1891 before beginning a steady decline to its present day figure. Employment prospects for school-leavers are bleak and most have to seek work on the mainland.

At the moment, fish-farming, the ferry, the estate, agriculture, cheese-making, and the fishing industry provide employment for a few. Some seasonal work is also available at the hotel.

Historically-speaking, Gigha was inhabited by the Picts as far back as the second century. However, at the beginning of the sixth century, the Picts were overwhelmed by the Dalriadic Scots but by the year 900 all the western isles had been conquered by the invading Norsemen, who were to rule for 400 years.

Gigha people were, by the 13th century, quite happy with the Norwegian occupation, despite the plundering of three centuries earlier. After all, the Norsemen caused less trouble than the Princes of Dalriada and their prime motives for retaining control of Gigha were the supply of timber, labour and, of course, a safe anchorage.

They also shared the same Christian religious beliefs and had a lot in common with the islanders through a combined fondness for song and verse. Also, the Gigha folk had little respect for the Scottish King, Alexander III. To them, he was an unknown quantity to whom no loyalty could be offered.

Gigha's history from the Norsemen's departure in 1266 until the end of the 18th century is curiously sketchy. In his 'The Story of Gigha', the late Sheriff J MacMaster-Campbell, a noted historian, wrote: "The record is strangely silent about Gigha – strange because of the high strategic value of the island lying, conveniently as it does, in the entirely navigable channel between Kintyre and the extensive island whose coastline so pleasantly interrupts the seascape to the traveller along the western seaboard of Argyll."

However, what is known is that, after centuries of clan rivalry and split ownership, Gigha was purchased outright as one unit in 1865 by J Williams Scarlett, the first of the modern lairds. Scarlett took possesion of the island for the sum of £49,000 and it was to remain in his family for more than 50 years. Successive proprietors have been Major John Allen; R J A Hamer; Somerset De Chair; Sir James Horlick; David Landale; Malcolm Potier and Derek Holt.

Great distress was caused on Gigha in 1992 when a huge business deal struck by the incumbent of the time, Malcolm Potier, went terribly wrong. The bankrupted Potier's assets, including Gigha, were seized and confusion reigned in the eight months following as the island stuttered from day to day under the control of a Swiss banking concern. Farm and tied house tenancies were threatened and estate affairs ground to a halt.

Not until September, when Gigha was bought by Mr Derek Holt, of Holt Leisure Parks, did any feeling of security return to the islanders.

The Ferry

The 100–foot car ferry 'Lochranza', resplendent in the Caledonian MacBrayne livery of black and white hull, red superstructure and buff masts, is the island's lifeline, linking it with Tayinloan on the Kintyre mainland. She was built at Hessle, near Hull, in 1987, one of a series of 'Loch' class vessels designed for the company to service the needs of some of the shorter west coast crossings.

These roll-on, roll-off ferries are somewhat unique in that they are not driven by propellers in the conventional manner but are fitted with German-designed Voith Schneider units. A series of blades, similar in shape to a cricket bat, protrude downwards from the ship's hull and are set diagonally opposite to each other fore and aft. Each Schneider is powered by a 320 hp Volvo diesel engine and gear box and the ship's momentum is controlled by a pitch lever on the bridge. Twin flat mounted steering wheels beside the pitch lever can also, if both turned to 90 degrees, drive the vessel sideways at a speed of four knots.

I serve, variously, as seaman purser, motorman and relief master on the 'Lochranza' and it came as something of a shock to my system when I first took the controls of the boat. After having spent 25 years handling single-screwed fishing vessels of anything up to 73 feet, I reckoned I had a fair idea of berthing procedure. End of story.

Being flat bottomed, the Loch class boats are very much at the mercy of the wind and tide, which can run with considerable strength in the Gigha Sound. It was very difficult for me to 'think Loch class' and not, say, 'Noble of Girvan' or 'Jones of Buckie' (fishing boat builders of repute); especially at the slipways when carrying out the berthing manoeuvre.

My 'Lochranza' tutors, John Bannatyne and Lachie Wotherspoon, were both carefree young gentlemen until given the task of showing me the ropes. Boys, I apologise to you both now for having aged you so much!

Winter time, naturally, sees a fair amount of service cancellations, perhaps not so much due to the sea state since 'Lochranza' in my opinion is an extremely stable ship, but because of the difficulty of cross winds at the slipways. Sometimes, on the weather shore, conditions appear to be fine, with the wind blowing off the land and little in the way of motion to be seen. However, it can be so very different three miles across the Sound on the lee shore.

I would like to think, though, that the service provided is a fairly good and efficient one, backed up by an onshore team headed by Ms Fay Thompson at the Kennacraig Ferry Terminal in West Loch Tarbert.

At the time of writing, the ferry is manned on a roster system by John Bannatyne, Lachie Wotherspoon, Alasdair McNeill, Willie McSporran, Johnnie Andrew and myself. The vessel is usually berthed at Gigha's South Pier and begins the daily service from the island slipway in Ardminish Bay. However, the South Pier is completely exposed to strong easterly winds and on such occasions 'Lochranza' must lie overnight at the Tayinloan jetty, which is sheltered from this direction. The crew keep sleeping equipment and spare clothes aboard for such emergencies and have the use of a modern, well-equipped galley/mess room.

Gigha, of course, has always had a ferry of some kind. As early as 1758, the Commissioners of Supply of Argyll decreed that money collected on the island should be used to construct a pier at Caolas Gigalum, the narrow strait which runs between Gigha and Gigalum islet. At the end of the eighteenth century, the Gigha ferryman was entitled to charge the following: one person, two shillings (10p); two or more, one shilling (5p) each until the number of passengers exceeded five. When this happened, the five shilling fare (25p) was shared by the number on board.

The Isle of Skye, in recent times, achieved universal notoriety by the actions of certain Free Church clergy attempting to stop the ferrying of passengers to and from the island on the Sabbath. That was nothing new on Gigha for, in 1799, two men were charged with Sabbath breaking by transporting oats from a local farm to Kilberry and Jura while Divine Service was in progress. Donald MacQuilkan, the ferryman, was declared blameless because he had been considerably pressured into carrying out the shameless deed.

The first steamer ever to call at Gigha was the 'Lochiel' in 1877. Before the long derelict pier at Caolas Gigalum was reconstructed in 1895, steamer passengers had to be ferried out by rowing boat.

Three small passenger ferries also ran between what is now Tayinloan and Gigha at that time.

It appears that the Ferry Croft, now a holiday cottage, was granted to one John Wotherspoon in 1885 on his appointment as ferryman by the owner of Gigha, Colonel W. J. Scarlett. John continued as ferryman until the outbreak of World War 1, though the terms and conditions of his employment as laid down by Scarlett seem to have been unreasonably harsh.

A 19-foot sailing boat named 'Broad Arrow' kept up the ferry service until the early 1940's, when Johnnie 'Beembo' Macmillan, often assisted by Graham McCulloch, operated two bonnie little wooden boats called the 'Village Belle' and the 'Jamie Boy', which were 26-feet and 22-feet-long respectively. Both were powered by the ubiquitous Kelvin petrol/paraffin engine and used the Achnaha tidal jetty in Ardminish Bay. This was later extended by a steel catwalk and nowadays serves as a convenient landing stage for visiting yachtsmen's dinghies and other small local craft.

Following the construction of a new landing stage at Tayinloan in the early sixties, the then Argyll County Council built a sturdy 28-foot clinker-planked boat and named her 'Shuna'. Her eventual skipper, Jura man Ian McKechnie, provided, at his own expense, a sister ship called 'Cara Lass'. Ian ran the ferry service for nearly 20 years.

In February, 1979, Caledonian MacBrayne inaugurated a daily car ferry service to Gigha from Kennacraig using the 'Island' class vessel, 'Bruernish', which was capable of carrying six vehicles. The service was opened up by Jimmy Cowie and Stewart Robertson, well-known in ferry circles, and was also crewed by popular figures such as Hughie Swanson and Donald 'Paraffin Dan' MacLean.

In May, 1979, command of the ferry was assumed by Campbeltown man James Robertson, later to become Assistant Personnel Manager at the company's Gourock headquarters.

James resided on Gigha and skippered the 'Bruernish' for the next 18 months, until the slipways and new approach roads on the island and across the water at Tayinloan were ready.

Before the construction of the slipways, vehicles had to be craned off the 'Bruernish' at the South Pier. Passengers had the option of using either the car ferry or the small wooden ferries which Ian still ran from Tayinloan until the discontinuation of the 'wee' boat service,when he was appointed skipper of the 'Bruernish'. He served until the 1980's, and was succeeded by Graham McCulloch. On Graham's retirement the reins were taken over by Archie Graham until 1996 when he, in turn, retired and the post was taken up by John Bannatyne. The 'Island' class 'Bruernish' was replaced by 'Lochranza' in 1992.

Of course, all through the years of the small ferry until the arrival of the bow-loading 'Bruernish', Gigha continued to be served by the larger ferries which plied the Islay and Jura route. The 'Pioneer' was an ancient paddle steamer which called at Gigha from 1905 until 1939, when she was replaced by the 'Lochiel'. The 'Lochiel' was followed by the lift-type car ferry 'Arran', which had been converted to roll on-roll off. The last big ferry to visit Gigha on a regular basis was the 'Pioneer', built in the 1970's.

The service, understandably, could be erratic as they called on alternate days only at the South Pier. The remaining days meant dropping anchor off the north end of the island to await the arrival of a punt launched from the shore. This small boat service was carried out for many years by Angus Wilkieson before being taken over by Seamus McSporran.

Stories emanating from the ferry service are many and varied and I would like to share a few of them with you, beginning with an experience I had shortly after joining Caledonian MacBrayne.

I was having bother understanding the complexities of the computerised ticket machine when a suave-looking Londoner in his thirties asked for a return ticket to Gigha. I fed the necessary information into the machine and awaited, with a silent prayer, the emergence of a ticket.

"Owd on a mineet, Jock. A'int this fing any good?" he asked as he flourished a London Transport bus pass.

"Not unless you want to cross the Serpentine," I answered.

There were about thirty passengers lined up behind this

Cockney gentleman and they began to show agitation at the delay. It took me about five minutes to convince him that a London Transport bus pass was anything but valid aboard a Caledonian MacBrayne western isles car ferry.

In the same vein, Lachie tells a story about a chap who, about to purchase a ticket on the 'Bruernish', asked the purser – who shall remain nameless – if he could have a disabled person's issue. Seeing no obvious signs of disability, the purser told the gentleman concerned, in a distinctly succinct manner, to stop mucking about and produce the full fare, which reluctantly he did. Minutes later, the man was seen to be having difficulty in ascending the wheelhouse stairway where, in some distress, he reported the matter to the skipper. It transpired that he was almost totally blind!

During the national seaman's strike of 1966, a Royal Navy minesweeper was deployed to carry essential goods to the islands and she dropped anchor off the north end of Gigha. Seamus McSporran had by this time taken over as north end ferryman and he was assisted on this occasion by the late Dugald McNeill. The minesweeper's captain had displayed a remarkable degree of caution by dropping his hook a long way offshore, a matter which annoyed Dugald greatly. As the little boat drew alongside the navyman he shouted up at the captain: "Do you see the distance between your boat and the land?"

When the skipper replied in the affirmative Dugald replied: "Well, there's ass much watter below yer boat ass there iss above it between you and the shore!"

The ebullient Captain Nisbet, of original 'Pioneer' fame, was noted for the respect he paid the fairer sex. On one occasion a crowd of young Gigha ladies from the church guild were gathered at the South Pier to await the arrival of the 'Pioneer' which was to take them on the first stage of an exciting journey to Glasgow.

Meanwhile, aboard the 'Pioneer', Captain Nisbet was becoming increasingly concerned about the behaviour of an Aberdeen Angus bull, which was to be put ashore on Gigha to service a herd, and he intimated he would be glad to see the back of it.

As the steamer approached the pier, where the band of young women thronged, Captain Nisbet leaned over the wind dodger and roared: "Iss there anyone here for the bull?"
Two gentlemen en route for their home island from West Loch

Tarbert aboard the old 'Pioneer' inadvertently walked past the purser's office. Seconds later a head appeared out of the hatch and a voice demanded: "Your dues, your dues," to which one of the men retorted: "We're bugger all of the kind. We're Gigha men."

Captain Willie John MacKinnon, one time master in the MacBrayne fleet, was renowned for his admirable seamanship. He sailed in weather that many a lesser man would have turned from and one of his attributes was close quarter ship handling. On one occasion he made an excellent job of taking a steamer alongside Gigha Pier during a violent storm.

When an islander later paid tribute to his skills, Captain MacKinnon replied: "Aye, it wass no' bad for a teenker's son, uhh?" His mother was, in fact, of tinker descent.

The 'Big Hoose'

Gigha was well-known to its present proprietor, Derek Holt, long before the debacle of 1992 which saw the island plunged into crisis through the failure of a business deal which bankrupted the then owner, Malcolm Potier.

As a keen sailor, Mr Holt spent many happy seagoing holidays cruising Scotland's west coast and he used the Ardminish Bay anchorage frequently as a base for runs ashore on the island.

A Lancashire man by birth, Mr Holt displayed good business acumen at an early age and he built up a notable empire in the world of leisure in Scotland, where the family has resided for 38 years. Probably his best-known success in yachting circles was the construction of the Inverkip Marina in Renfrewshire, the first in Scotland. His company, Holt Leisure, also owns other yachting centres and caravan parks and he is reputed to have paid about £2million for Gigha when it was forced on to the market.

Before coming to Gigha, Mr Holt owned Skibo Castle, near Dornoch, in Sutherland. He and his wife, June, have three daughters, the youngest of whom, Sandra, and her husband, William Howden, an Easter Ross man, reside on the island and look after the day to day running of the estate and any ancillary business.

Now in his sixties, Mr Holt spends as much time as possible on Gigha, which he regards as home, and also visits South Africa, where he has a keen interest in racehorses. He has represented Scotland competitively at his other passion of sports fishing.

The laird's seat on Gigha, Achamore House, was originally known as the Mansion House and was built in two stages, firstly by John McNeill in the late 1700's. It was extended extensively in 1884 but three years after Yorke Scarlett's ascendancy to the lairdship, in 1893, a horrendous fire destroyed the top storey.

On the day of the blaze, the Scarlett family were off the island and the servants were playing golf at the Leim course. The first man to spot the conflagration was Sandy Orr, a local grocer and shoemaker, as he drove his pony and trap towards the South Pier. Sandy later penned a short poem about the incident which ran:

> *I lowsed the horse oot o' the cart,*
> *I galloped to the shore,*
> *I cried out to the golfers,*
> *There's flames at Achamore.*
>
> *I jumped into the passages,*
> *So loudly did I roar,*
> *There's flames at Achamore, boys,*
> *There's flames at Achamore.*

Much of the furniture and silver was saved by the butler and servants on their speedy return from the golf course. Renovation work commenced immediately but it was decided not to rebuild the badly damaged top storey and the house was re-roofed accordingly.

A Gigha brochure published in 1911 highlighted Achamore House's graphic singularity and chronicled with pride the spacious entrance hall and lavishly carved banisters on the wide stairways. It also tells of the many oak-panelled walls in the downstairs rooms, the raw material for which must have been shipped in. The cleverly designed house features both mullion and deep sash windows which let the light play upon the well-appointed and individually unique rooms.

A total of 16 staff, ranging from butler to nursemaid, were employed at the house in the early 1900's. Visiting ladies and gentlemen were accompanied by their maids and valets.

Water for washing and bathing had to be carried to all the bedrooms and more than 40 lamps of all kinds had to be cleaned, trimmed and filled with paraffin each day.

Dining was an experience to behold, with the day's culinary delights being rounded off by a six-course dinner in the evening.

Life at Achamore House throughout the years under the various lairds remained pretty well unchanged, save for the universal reduction in domestic staff, until the arrival of David

Landale in 1973. The house was let to holidaymakers – well-heeled holidaymakers that is – for anything up to a month at a time. Pheasant shooting parties were also catered for during the winter months.

The last proprietor, Malcolm Potier, attempted to further Landale's scheme by converting the house into a conference centre, the idea being to attract jaded businessmen from high pressure city life to the serenity of Gigha. Extensive fire safety precautions such as an alarm system and special doors were installed along with a comprehensive telephone system covering all rooms.

However, the plan, to host short business/pleasure breaks, was badly hit by the recession and never really got off the ground.

Today, the house is used solely for residential and office purposes on a year round basis by William and Sandra Howden and by Mr and Mrs Holt. The large kitchen has been re-converted into a room for domestic, rather than commercial use.

The house stands surrounded by 50 of the most gloriously cultivated acres to be found anywhere, the famous Achamore Gardens. They are said to be among the finest of their kind in Britain and contain plants of incalculable value.

Holt Leisure Parks and the National Trust for Scotland, which owns a plant collection within the semi-tropical gardens, jointly manage this horticulturalist's paradise. Islander Malcolm MacNeill, of Keill, is head gardener.

It was the late Sir James Horlick, the highly regarded owner of Gigha between 1944 and 1972, who was responsible for the laying down of the gardens. He achieved in 25 years what would normally have taken several successive generations of learned and devoted gardeners, thanks to his wealth of knowledge on the subject.

Sir James actually first ventured to the Scottish west coast to inspect an estate on Islay which was on the market. Unimpressed, he looked over another in north Argyll which did not meet his requirements either. It was there, by pure chance, that he heard of the Isle of Gigha, extending to 3,560 acres, was for sale. Not long afterwards he was in residence, having taken an immediate liking to the island.

The woodlands surrounding Achamore House were planted about one hundred years ago to provide cover for game. Sir James added further windbreaks and the benefits were obvious within a few years. It is difficult to imagine when strolling through the gardens, the silence interrupted only by the call of a peacock or some other wild fowl, that one is actually on a Scottish island.

Sir James was an avid admirer of rhododendrons and the background to the Achamore gardens is formed by no fewer than seven different species, including the 'Horlick hybrids'. Scattered throughout the rest of the gardens are exotic plants such as azalea, camellia, magnolia, hydrangea and viburnum, to name but a few. There are also many foreign semi-tropical species from origins including Chile, Australasia, Mexico, California and Thailand.

The woodland is made up of sycamore, beech, elm, ash, chestnut, larch and Scots pine. Sir James added to this by introducing rowan, whitebeam and ornamental trees in open clearings.

Ideal growing conditions in the shade and moistness of the low woodland encourage herbaceous plants such as primula, native primrose, meconoposis, kniphofia, blue Himalayan poppy and waterside iris.

Gigha's favourable climate is a boon to the gardener, providing there is adequate wind shelter. Its annual average rainfall of 45 inches is in no way excessive and the North Atlantic Drift current in winter ensures that the temperature does not fluctuate wildly. Severe frosts are unusual with anything more than 10 degrees of frost considered a rarity.

The soil at Achamore varies from being light sandy loam on the hillside, easily drained because of the underlying gravel, to the heavy lower woodland earth. It is highly acid apart from the walled garden where cultivation and liming over a long period have created a fertile soil.

The signposted route around the gardens extends to a distance of about two miles but this covers the main areas only. Sir James created gardens within the gardens and it would take a long time to visit the clearings not readily noticeable off the recognised path.

The gardens are a joy to look at any time, but undoubtedly at their best towards the end of May and in early June, when an absolute riot of colour is guaranteed.

Fishing Lore

Perhaps a little surprisingly, Gigha has only two commercial fishing vessels of any size, despite its strategic position in relation to the frequently lucrative prawn and scallop grounds in the vicinity of the island.

There are, however, several smaller inshore creel boats which pursue species such as lobster, brown crab, velvet crab and 'buckie' whelks, the latter being sought for export to Malaysian concerns, where they are regarded as a delicacy.

The two boats which presently fish for prawns and scallops on a seasonal basis are the 'Mari-Dor' (BA 217) and the 'Green Isle' (B 80).

The 'Mari-Dor' is skipper-owned by Archie MacAlister and is manned by himself and two crewmen. Built by MacKay Boatbuilders, of Arbroath, in 1970, the vessel is a traditional beamy 40-footer of Scottish design and she is powered by a 172hp Gardner diesel engine, a marine unit famed for reliability. The crew is assisted greatly in the retrieval of the fishing gear by a heavy-duty trawl winch and power block, both of which are hydraulically operated.

Gigha's other trawler, the 'Green Isle', is owned by the Wilkieson brothers, John Ronald and Robin, who run the vessel successfully themselves, 'JR' being skipper. She was built in Cornwall during 1988 by Cygnus Marine, a firm which specialises in the quality construction of boats in GRP (glass reinforced plastic). Although the 'Green Isle' is just 37-feet long, her layout with forward wheelhouse gives the impression of a much larger boat. Her engine is also a Gardner of 127hp and the trawl winch and telescopic net crane are also run by hydraulics. The Wilkieson brothers have the added bonus of being able to turn to creel fishing on a big scale should the need arise as she is also fitted out for such operations.

In the late fifties, two Campbeltown herring ring-netters, the 'Margaret Rose' (CN 115) and the 'Boy Danny' (CN 142) were, in common with all other herring boats, experiencing a slump in the fishery. Their experiments with prawn nets on the grounds around Gigha sparked off a huge seasonal fishing which has continued to maintain its viability to this day. Big fleets of boats from the Clyde, Oban and even the east coast, have used Gigha and Port Ellen, on Islay, as a base whilst participating in the fishery.

As the years passed, prawn trawlers became more and more efficient and the type of engines which drove the 'Margaret Rose' and 'Boy Danny' – 114hp Gardner and 88hp Kelvin respectively – were replaced with modern high-revving units from the likes of Caterpillar, Volvo and Cummins. Indeed, the peace and quiet of many a tranquil July evening at Gigha's South Pier has been shattered by the combined engine noise of anything up to 30 boats as the crews bent to the laborious task of tailing huge heaps of small prawns taken from the infamous 'Sou'-west o' Cara' grounds.

This was one part of my fishing career which holds no fond memories whatsoever and I can put my hand on my heart and say that I do not miss it in the slightest. How I hated having to sit on the boat's rail, back aching and wrist swollen, looking at a veritable 'haystack' of small scampi-sized prawns, every one of which had to be tailed in readiness for the market. I often sat down at 2am to a dinner which should have been eaten the previous evening! But, of course, when all said and done, there was money in it.

Massive scallop beds were also found in the waters close to Gigha in 1966, when several boats from Kirkcudbright, on the Solway Firth, arrived. Daily catches of 80 and 90 hundredweight (50kg) bags of clams were frequently made in the early days and Skipper John King, a legendary scallop fisherman who pioneered much of the efficient gear in use today, took a tremendous catch of 101 bags in a mere eight hours while in command of the 'Ranger'.

So why did the men of Gigha fail to take advantage of this fishing bonanza?

Iain Wilkieson, a fit-looking man who, at 72 still fishes for lobster and crab in a 16-foot boat, reckons that the islanders "hadn't got the push" when it came to approaching financial institutions for the much-needed backing required for such ventures. Sadly, he says, it is too late now. This can be borne out by the fact that Archie MacAlister is heavily reliant on Campbeltown fishermen to crew his boat, though his son Neil has now left school to join him on the board.

Iain began fishing full-time in the mid-fifties and, in 1960, joined Graham McCulloch aboard the 33-foot 'Speedwell', a Kelvin-engined lobster and scallop boat which was built in Mallaig. He fished with Graham for 15 years before purchasing the 34-foot scalloper 'Girl Aileen' from a Campbeltown owner. Following a successful reign as skipper he handed over command to John Ronald a few years ago. The 88 hp Lister-powered 'Girl Aileen' was replaced by the 'Green Isle' in 1995.

Iain told me, however, that Gigha's fishermen enjoyed fairly good times from around 1930 until the outbreak of the last world war, when the fleet consisted of six Loch Fyne skiffs and a large launch-type boat.

The skiffs were built of larch on oak construction in various Firth of Clyde yards. They were fitted out with forward foc'sle accommodation for four, two in bunks and two on seat lockers which doubled up as beds. Heat was provided by a 'Jack Tar' coal fire and cooking was done on the popular Primus paraffin stove. Life was, if reasonably well rewarded, tough for the men of the Gigha fleet. Cod lines were set, using anything up to 900 shellfish-baited hooks, from the last days of January until the end of April. Fish which could not be sold fresh were dried and salted, after which the boats set sail for places such as Oban, Port Ellen and Ayr to market them.

The lobster fishing season was perhaps hardest on the men of Gigha, in that the fishery was carried on in waters away from home. Bad weather sometimes meant a prolonged period of separation from loved ones.

The skiffs left Gigha on a Monday morning, each one towing a 17-foot 'mini' skiff and a punt. The lobster pots were carried in the big boat, along with provisions, fresh water, bait and so on. Favoured haunts of the Gigha fishermen were the MacCormick Islands, particularly Eilean Mor, situated just west of Loch Sween. They also fished at Chuirn Island, near Islay, the Islay shore and the Jura shore.

The crews lived aboard the main skiff while the smaller boats were used for actual fishing operations, being able to get in and out of shallow, rocky inlets safely.

It is ironic to think that species such as velvet crab and 'buckie' whelks, which are sought so eagerly nowadays, were considered a real nuisance by the Gigha lobstermen. Quite valueless, the crabs and whelks would often eat the bait before the prized lobster could get near. Just how many tonnes of 'jessocks' – to give the velvet crab its Gigha name – were jettisoned over the years is difficult to imagine but the mind boggles when one considers their present day value of £2.00 per kilo!

Hopefully, the men would be able to return to Gigha on Saturday mornings and attend Sunday church service but there were occasions when they could be absent for weeks due to the inclemency of the weather. Crinan was used as a haven during the enforced exiles and although it is a fairly short road journey from there to Tayinloan, the men would still have been unable to cross the storm-tossed Gigha Sound.

The 'Jessie Jane' was a 35-footer which belonged to James and John McNeill. She was principally engaged in herring drifting, cod longlining and lobster potting, and carried, in addition to her owners, a further two crewmen. The 'Jessie Jane' was powered by a 15/20 Kelvin engine.

Incredibly, this vessel, which was built in 1911, is still going strong and called at Gigha on August 20, 1996. Her present owner, who uses the 'Jessie Jane' for pleasure cruising around the UK, had no idea that the boat provided a living for four Gigha fishermen during her working life.

The 'Molly Dhonn', another 35-foot skiff, belonged to John Wotherspoon. She was fitted with an 8/10 Kelvin and fished for cod and lobsters. Her normal complement of two men was supplemented by a further two when engaged in the longline fishery.

The 'Robina' was owned by John Ronald MacDonald, for whom the skipper of the 'Green Isle' is called. She was a 34-footer and was also driven by an 8/10 Kelvin.

Dugald and Donnie McNeill's boat was called the 'Renown'. This 35-footer had a 15/20 Kelvin for propulsion and they concentrated mainly on lobster fishing.

31

The lobsters were the mainstay, also, of brothers Duncan and Malcolm McNeill, who owned and operated the 'Janet'. This boat was slightly smaller than the rest at 32 feet and her power came, similarly, from a Kelvin 8/10.

The 'Style' was the proud possession of Peter MacCallum. This 34-footer was fitted with yet another Kelvin 8/10 but had the added luxury of a gearbox to enable her to go astern, thus easing berthing difficulties. The 'Style' also fished solely for lobsters.

The 'Lady Belle' was Johnnie 'Beembo' Macmillan's boat. Despite the fact that she was built along launch lines and was the smallest, at 28 feet, this did not deter Beembo from taking part in the cod fishery as well as lobster potting. She was crewed by three men whilst cod fishing and her power came from a Kelvin 12/14. Beembo landed an astonishing 461 lobsters for one week's work during the month of August, 1945. At present day prices this would represent approximately £5000!

The longevity of the Gigha boats can be further demonstrated by the presence of a punt which was built 104 years ago and is still in everyday use. It was built by Iain Wilkieson's grandfather, who made a living on the island as a boatbuilder, turning out skiffs of up to 20 feet in length.

Iain tells how the outbreak of the second world war was instrumental in bringing about the decline of the Gigha fishing industry, when all sorts of restrictions were imposed on the movement of boats and, of course, the inevitable call-up of young men.

My 'Lochranza' shipmate, Alasdair McNeill, was brought up in a fishing household, his father being Duncan McNeill, of the 'Janet'. Alasdair, one of a family of seven, opted for a career in the army, where he spent 25 years before returning to his native isle. But he remembers with affection an extremely happy childhood as a fisherman's son spent by the shoreline at Tigh Na Rhuda. The family perhaps did not live amid trappings of luxury but they never wanted for anything and there was no lack of love in the home.

Alasdair reflects: "I wish everyone could have such happy formative years as I had. My childhood memories are joyous indeed."

Alasdair's brother, John, spent a lifetime hunting lobsters and , although he was forced into semi-retirement following surgery, still works a 16-foot boat and about 30 creels.

Angus McVean, Gigha's oldest resident　　*Graham McCulloch*

The former open decked ferry 'Jamie Boy', which Graham McCulloch painstakingly converted into a cabin cruiser

Achamore House, home to a succession of Gigha proprietors for many years

The Gigha School role call. Mrs Lorna MacAlister with her 12 pupils of varying ages

Gigha School's centenary celebrations and Victoriana exhibition

The Michelle-Anne', a 19-foot lobster/crab potter operated single-handedly by Keith Helm, at her south pier mooring

Ian Wilkieson and 'crew' on board the punt which celebrated its 100th birthday a few years ago.

MFV's 'Green Isle' (B 80) and 'Mari-Dor' alongside at Gigha's south pier

MFV 'Mari-Dor' steaming through Gigha Harbour en route to land at Tayinloan

Gigha and Cara Parish Church, built as recently as 1923, is fitted with several stunning stained glass windows

Ruins of the 13th century Kilchattan Church

The Hangman's Stone

The original 'JR' in 1952

Malcolm MacNeill, head gardener, Achamore House

Alastair Brown, greenkeeper at Gigha Golf Club

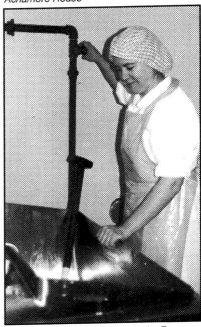

Sheila McNeill in the dairy at Leim Farm

In reflective mood, William McSporran, presides as chairman over regular Community Council meetings on Gigha;

Gigha's HM Coastguard Auxiliary-in-charge John Martin, of Burnside, talking by radio to headquarters in Greenock;

The present day fishermen of Gigha have a lifestyle far removed from their pre-war predeccessors. It is rare, indeed, for either Archie or JR to stray far from home waters, which is a good thing because they do not have to. They work seasonally at whatever may be going and it is only in cases of extreme scarcity that they venture either through the Sound of Islay to the Colonsay waters, or round the Mull of Kintyre to the Clyde prawn fishery.

Their boats are comprehensively equipped with electronic navigation and detection gadgetry which, along with the comfortable onboard living conditions, would have JR's namesake scratching his head in bewilderment.

Landings are made at Tayinloan on a daily basis each evening and the lads enjoy the luxury of being able to go home at night. This method of working does not in any way detract from their ability as fishers of the sea and the job is carried out in a competent manner. In fact, if some of the greedier fishermen elsewhere followed their example the state of the industry nationally might well be in better shape.

As always, there were characters at the fishing whose presence could lighten the hearts of all around, especially if the weather was bad or if there was a dearth of fish. One such man was Hector MacQuilkan, whose ability to convert any topic quickly into verse was astonishing.

The lobsters were pretty thin on the grounds and Hector was given the opportunity of earning a few shillings by ferrying a party of tourists on a day trip to neighbouring Cara. The holidaymakers were headed by a condescending individual called Professor Montgomery, a man who took a bizarre delight in belittling Hector on the journey across. When he stepped ashore on Cara in the glorious sunshine of a summer's morn he said to Hector: "Harrumph. I'll bet nobody has ever thought of composing a piece of poetry about this place." The professor was poleaxed when Hector retorted instantaneously:

It's now the month of August in 1934,
With Montgomery as our skipper to the haunted isle we go,
Where nature paints a picture that no artist can excel,
The majestic Paps of Jura, with their ancient look of yore,
The Atlantic billows surging round my native island's shore.

Professor Montgomery was silenced.

A group of fishermen were sitting around in the shelter of a shed at Gallochoille, at the south end of Ardminish Bay, when one of them noticed a small barrel being swept along by wind and tide. A rescue operation was put into immediate effect and the cask was retrieved from the briny.

The men's delight was complete when, on the removal of the bung, it was seen to contain a few gallons of best whisky. The only suitable receptacle to hand was a galvanised pail and the contents were poured into this as the men gathered round. One of their number, Bob McMillan, lifted the pail to his head and announced with glee: "Noo for a bloody good bucket."

A true story I have told elsewhere in print concerning whisky and fishing comes to mind and I don't mind repeating it here.

I was working with Skipper Alec Burnfield aboard the Campbeltown trawler 'Nostaw' (SN 48) in the summer of 1989. Alec was a great exponent of the Gigha prawn fishery and, weather permitting, could be found there at any season of the year but the day in question was one of perfect sunshine and calm, with an azure sea shimmering below a fiery sun. Ideal conditions, yes, but the unfortunate fact was that the prawns were reluctant to leave their seabed burrows, resulting in a poor day's fishing.

At the completion of the last haul of the day, just off the western approach to Gigha harbour, our pessimism was once more fully justified when the cod end was seen to float to the surface, a sure sign of an empty net. However, as we went through the motions of releasing the minimal contents of the trawl, Alec and I looked at one another with incredulity when a beautiful three-pound lobster and an unopened 40-ounce bottle of The Famous Grouse whisky dropped on to the deck.

Now, Alec is well-known as a bit of a prankster and a master of the wind-up and when he reported our extraordinary catch to other skippers on the radio nobody would believe him. However, the 'catch' was displayed that night at Gigha's South Pier for all to see.

Yet another story emanating from the Gigha fishing industry and whisky concerns John Ronald MacDonald, mentioned earlier as skipper-owner of the 'Robina'. On this occasion he and a crewman were fishing for lobsters in his other boat, the 17-foot skiff, 'Marion'.

It was in the early 1930's and Gigha was rising in popularity with yachstmen as an ideal base for west coast cruising. It appears that one of them got into difficulties and John Ronald saved the day by getting the stricken yacht to a safe anchorage. Offers of payment were forthcoming but the Gigha men's code in those days eschewed the acceptance of money under such circumstances.

The following day, when checking the lobster pots, John Ronald and his crewman were flabbergasted to find a half-gallon flask of whisky jammed into one of the creels when it was hauled to the surface. It transpired that the yachtsmen, determined to acknowledge their thanks, had found out where the gear was set and had sneaked out to the spot to deposit their token of appreciation.

The brothers Donald, Calum and Neil Smith, who worked one of the Drumeonbeg crofts, led a life similar to many Scots crofters of their time. They tended a few head of cattle, kept a horse, a few sheep and some chickens as well as raising a limited amount of crops. Their farming income was augmented by lobster fishing in the summer and autumn.

One particularly successful fishing trip resulted in a good catch of the valuable crustaceans and their haul included a lobster of sizeable proportions. Donald mentioned this to a friend and, as happens in small communities the world over, the dimensions of the lobster increased until it had reached gargantuan proportions. Lobsters then, as now, survive for a considerable time in 'keep' boxes anchored close inshore until marketing conditions are favourable, and a few weeks elapsed before the Smith brothers decided to consign their catch to London's Billingsgate Market.

The transhipping method at that time was to pack the lobsters in salt water-impregnated sawdust in order to ensure their survival during the long journey south. When Calum appeared at the village with several boxes for forwarding to the South Pier to await the West Loch Tarbert ferry, several inquisitive islanders demanded to be shown the huge lobster. Catching on immediately, Calum replied: "Och, that yin. It'll be here in a wee while. Neil's chust takin' it doon the road on a lead!"

The Smiths were prone to exaggerate matters but they surely overstepped the mark when someone asked them about the supposedly huge pig they had reared. Donald replied: "Aye, it wass some size right enough. In fact we used its ears to make a new lugsail for the boat.

Down on the Farm

Johnnie Andrew, my friend and shipmate on the 'Lochranza', left school in 1958 to work at Gigha's Leim Farm for the princely sum of 30 shillings (£1.50) per week. Let's face it, that year was hardly in the Dark Ages but it was before there was such a thing as a minimum basic wage in agriculture and farmers could pay labourers whatever they wished.

For his "therty bob", the 15-years-old Johnnie worked a 10-hour day Monday to Friday and five hours on Saturday. The highlight of his week in those days was a visit with his young friends to the South Pier on Saturday afternoons to await the arrival of the mail steamer!

Johnnie was to spend the next thirty years as a farmworker, chiefly with Bob Blackwood at North Ardminish and Ardlamy, where, apart from carrying out normal farm duties, he developed considerable mechanical skills. Now he is never happier than when prowling around the 'Lochranza's' engine room in Caledonian MacBrayne boiler suit and bright yellow ear muffs. Does he miss the farming scene, which has shrunk so considerably on Gigha in recent years?

"Not a bit. Well, apart from the tractors," he says. When Johnnie began his agricultural journey there were eleven farms providing work for 42 people on the island. Of that figure, 16 were hired hands. In addition there were two full-time 'freelance' contractors who took on general jobs such as draining and fencing.

Nowadays, only the farms of Tarbert, Drumeonmore, Achamore, South Drumachro, Leim and Ardlamy continue as working units. However, at the time of writing, they are completely family-run by 14 people and, with the exception of an occasional dairyman at Leim, do not employ outside labour.

The lands of five others – North Ardminish, South Ardminish, Drumeonbeg, Kinererach and Achavenish – have, for a variety of reasons, been swallowed up by the remaining farmers or for other use, though the houses and steadings are still occupied by tenants.

Johnnie remembers, also, having to turn out on cold Saturday and Sunday mornings throughout the winter to feed hill cattle. It was not uncommon, either, for farmers to 'lend' their labour to neighbours and he was often sent to other places to help out.

Although the farmworkers were treated to two daily teabreaks and a midday meal, Johnnie discounts the stories often quoted about agricultural employees having access to all the milk, eggs, butter, potatoes and chickens they could eat. This was a mistaken belief, he says, and in fact he used to buy any potatoes he took home.

Farmworkers in general, and not just on Gigha, used to compare details of good and bad 'feeding' farmhouses, where wholesome fare was served or, indeed, the contrary. This reminds me of a true story involving a Gigha ploughman who was asked to assist at a farm where the farmer had fallen ill and was in hospital, leaving only his wife and a young maid to attend to things.

'Dinner' was served in the farmhouse at 1pm and the first day's meal consisted of a helping of salt herring and potatoes, for which the ploughman thanked the maid as she cleared away his plate. Encouraged by his reaction, the farmer's wife decided to give him the same food a second time and was delighted when he made no comment to the maid, although he appeared to have enjoyed his meal.

"I have a big barrel of salt herring and plenty of potatoes. This man is going to be easily fed," commented the woman on the third day as she prepared a similar repast.

This time, when the maid entered to clear the table the ploughman, with bowed head, mumbled almost inaudibly into his beard: "Hebrew, chapter thirteen, verse eight."

Puzzled, she reported the man's comment to her mistress, who in turn immediately reached for the family bible, consulted the appropriate text, and was much grieved to read: "Jesus Christ. The same yesterday, today and forever."

Apart from a well earned two week annual holiday, Johnnie's only other breaks were one-day visits to the Kintyre Agricultural Show held at Campbeltown in June and Tarbert Fair later in the summer.

Repetitive farm work, I suppose, can be tedious and this is borne out by the story Johnnie told me about an interesting experience he had one day after being asked to harrow a field. To the uneducated, harrowing a field is a process which involves towing a broad rake-like structure behind a tractor over ground that has been newly ploughed. This treatment breaks up and flattens the soil in readiness for sowing seed.

On the day in question, Johnnie's task took place in a particularly big field and the monotony of driving the tractor slowly from one end to the other eventually overcame him and he dropped quietly off to sleep. His nap was interrupted only when his Fordson Major made contact with a drystane dyke!

The annual Gigha Ploughing Match was an important date in the island's agricultural calendar, though it was discontinued a few years ago. It was a real fun day for the farming fraternity and when the serious business of ploughing and judging ended a much more light-hearted atmosphere, no doubt generated by liberal partaking of Scotia's national drink, entered the proceedings. Many of the participants continued the revelry in the hotel and I am reminded of an incident which occurred there on a ploughing match night in 1978 shortly after the hostelry re-opened after extensive and expensive renovations.

The gentleman concerned was obviously in dire need of his bed after reducing the level of a whisky bottle in the bar to an alarming extent. However, rather than make for home, a fair distance off, he decided on alternative accommodation in one of the hotel's exquisitely appointed bedrooms, the only problem being that he did not bother to tell anyone. Bear in mind that our friend had been at a ploughing match and would hardly be suitably attired for such sumptuous surroundings. He awoke early next morning, fully-clothed in bed with a terrible hangover, to the sound of the milk tanker filling up at a nearby byre. His unobserved – so he thought – escape was made good on the vehicle thanks to the sympathetic driver, Neil Bannatyne, who got him home in time for work. A few days later, however, the man was mortified when he received an official bed and breakfast bill signed by mine host of the time, Ken Roebuck. When he perceived that the bill was a good-natured 'wind-up' the merry ploughman had a lawyer friend reply to the hotel to say that since, in his opinion the accommodation was sub-standard, he would be withholding payment.

Another big night on Gigha which has carried on to this day, although not quite as riotously, are the festivities following the annual cattle sale, usually held at Achamore Farm.

The sale is conducted by Mr Robbie Wilson, who is connected to the firm of A & J Wilson, well-known in auctioneering circles for many years. The cattle are transported in floats aboard 'Lochranza' on the day following the sale but not so long ago it was a very different story.

Before the inauguration of the ro-ro ferry the cows bound for the mainland had to be assembled at the South Pier where they were loaded via a cattle ramp on to a special ferry. Sometimes problems arose en route and Gigha on cattle sale days had a distinctive 'Rawhide' look about it. Everyone prayed for a quick deluge of rain to wash away the evidence deposited by the big herd on the road and in the area of the pier!

There were, naturally, incidents involving the animals and on one occasion a bull fell into the water. It was successfully rescued, however, and came ashore in a little sandy bay on the west side of the pier.

Johnnie also told me of the time when 40 suckled calves were sold from Ardlamy and left Gigha on the MV 'Arran', a steamer of the MacBrayne fleet. At the head of West Loch Tarbert, two of the animals escaped and jumped into the sea. They swam across the loch and got ashore safely on the other side, whereupon they made good their escape. It was not until a week later that the calves were found at Kilberry, a long way off.

Probably the most important event to take place on Gigha in yesteryear was the annual Agricultural Show, formerly held in the paddock at the Home Farm, now known as Achamore. The field is still referred to on the island as the 'show field' though many a year has passed since there was such an occasion. In the early 1900's, Gigha's proprietor Mr William Scarlett used his yacht, 'Snapshot', to bring a pipe band across and many other visitors attended from all over the county of Argyll. The paddle steamer 'Pioneer' was chartered to do an extra run to cope with the influx of visitors.

I have just finished reading through a catalogue printed for

Gigha Agricultural Society by the Argyllshire Herald, Campbeltown, which refers to the summer show of 1905. There are no fewer than 20 exhibitors, including the Rev J.F.McKenzie, who had livestock in the church glebe, and John Wotherspoon, the ferryman who also worked Ferry Croft as part of his employment deal.

Although the main part of the show was the parade and judging, opportunist buyers of cattle and horses went round the farms to inspect stock and considerable business was done in this way. There were a further two farms, Highfield and Cairnvickoye, and three crofts in operation during this period.

Horses, naturally, featured strongly in farming circles for many years and Gigha farms normally had at least four, sometimes more. Some of the farmers exhibited at the Campbeltown Show, which meant a sea trip on the 'Pioneer' followed by a gruelling 36-mile walk from West Loch Tarbert to the town.

Once a year stallions were taken to Gigha to service the mares and apparently one of the men accompanying the horses had more than a passing interest in the ladies. So much so that an island woman once commented wryly: "Och, him, he left more on Gigha than the stallion did!"

Working collie dogs have always been part of farming life and individual animals often come under scrutiny from interested parties. Peter MacDonald, late of Drumeonmore Farm and his friend, Archie Bannatyne, who was tenant of Tarbert Farm, were having a Saturday night discussion on the merits of various sheepdogs. Peter told Archie that he had read an article in 'Scottish Farmer' praising the performance of one particularly able dog which, on being sent out by its master, could round up sheep sucessfully from a distance of more than a mile. Archie paused for a moment and stroked his whisker before commenting: "Och, that's nothin', Peter. I sent oot a dog a week ago an' the bugger hasna come back yet."

Modern day farmers on Gigha concentrate on dairying, taking full advantage of the lush pasture which covers so much of the island. Some 7000 litres of milk – 5000 in the winter months – are collected daily from five farms by a Bibby International milk tanker, the exception being Leim Farm, where cheese is made. Bibby International has a contract to supply the creamery in Campbeltown, which produces a popular high quality cheddar available nationwide on the shelves of such supermarkets as Tesco.

The highly successful husband and wife team of Jimmy and Olive Robinson have recently retired from the tenancy of Achamore, formerly the Home Farm. Originally from the Dumfries area, they moved to Gigha, after much soul searching, more than 20 years ago.

Slightly apprehensive they may have been then but, as Jimmy freely admits, they have, from humble beginnings, prospered on Gigha and spent many happy years on the island.

"This place has been good to us. A combination of hard work and the first class farming land of Gigha has made it all worthwhile. When I'm finished here I'm finished farming," says Jimmy.

They have now bought another farm, Oakwood Hill, at Canonbie, near Gretna, which is worked by their son, David. It was obvious after a few years at their first Gigha farm, Drumeonbeg, that they were going to make a go of things, though there were only 50 acres of arable and 86 acres of rough pasture. When the tenancy of the larger Achamore Farm – 121 arable and 92 rough – came up about 11 years ago they jumped at the chance.

Jimmy and Olive milked 70 cows twice daily, giving an average yield of 1000 litres of milk. They had a further 120 head of cattle, split between beef and dairy calves, since they reared their own replacement milkers.

Crops were restricted to 10 acres of barley and grass for grazing or making winter silage, though they had a sizeable vegetable patch for home consumption. The farm was well-equipped with all sorts of modern machinery, including a combine harvester which was hired out when not in use at Achamore.

One old-fashioned tradition they clung to was the production of home made butter, the tasty creaminess of which I can personally testify.

On the delicate subject of BSE, Jimmy reckons that the problem will end sooner, rather than later. He concedes there are many theories surrounding the origin of the disease, but he thinks the problem is a hereditary one through breeding, rather than being caused by feeding.

"I would say the end of BSE will come a lot quicker than folk actually think," he says.

Another form of 'farming' is thriving on Gigha, at the Drumeon Bay site of Gigha Fishfarms salmon breeding cages. This operation began in 1986 and is now run by Aquascot, an Alness-based concern.

The permanent full-time workforce of four, headed by Duncan McNeill, annually raise around 100,000 salmon weighing about 300 tonnes. The smolts are flown by helicopter to Gigha once a year and some 390 tonnes of feeding are used to fatten the fish to the ideal marketing weight of 3 kg – between six and seven pounds.

Two harvests take place each year and half a dozen temporary staff are taken on to assist in the gutting, cleaning and packing of the fish before being sent to Aquascot's headquarters for processing.

The finished product is marketed widely in Europe, but an important UK customer is the Marks and Spencer chain. Another fish farming development on Gigha has not been so lucky, though. An investment of nearly £3 million in a landsite turbot rearing farm ended disastrously a few years ago when 80,000 fish, affected by the VHS fish disease, had to be slaughtered and the plant closed down.

The good news, however, at the time of writing, is that a powerful business consortium are taking over the site and intend to resume farming turbot, cod and halibut, with the creation of possibly 10 valuable jobs.

V. T

Kirk Matters

The church on Gigha, in common with that in every other parish in Scotland, played an important part in the daily life and times of the island in days of yore.

These days, however, the worrying nationwide downward spiral in church attendances has not missed Gigha . A hard core of around 20 people, or one sixth of the population, regularly attend Sunday morning service in Gigha Parish Church, which stands in a commanding position overlooking Ardminish Bay on Cnocan a' Chiuil. The small but exquisite building is Gigha's fourth church and was constructed as recently as 1923 to replace the previous place of worship which stood directly opposite the hotel a few hundred yards distant. Indeed, much of the black whinstone from the old church was used by the builders.

Gigha, as can be imagined, is a haven of peace and quiet which is further emphasised on entering the church. One has only to look at the large number of entries and comments in the visitor's book to witness the appreciation of so many.

A fund for the badly needed renewal of the church building was inaugurated before the outbreak of World War 1 but had to be put on hold until hostilities ceased. The Consecration cross and the date are situated on the north wall of the chancel.

Once inside, one is immediately aware of the radiance generated by the glorious colours of the eight stained glass windows, surely unequalled in such a small church. Remembered in the windows are Sir James Horlick; Rev Donald MacFarlane (1907-1923); Margaret McNeill; Jennie McNeill; Annie Galbraith and Gigha servicemen who fell in action during both World Wars.

One of the most stunning is in memory of the Rev Kenneth MacLeod, DD, the much esteemed minister on Gigha from 1923 until 1948. His window shows David, adorned in crimson robes and gold crown, playing a clarsach. Smaller illustrations highlight St Brigid and her cow, St Patrick, St Columba's coracle and a scene depicting the Sound of Gigha.

The ancient baptisimal font, into which fits a hand-beaten Scottish silver bowl, was brought from the ruined church of Kilchattan. Communion today is celebrated using two silver goblets but there are still two large pewter communion cups, each with more than a pint capacity, in the church safe. These cups were made in the year 1795 along with pewter communion tokens, one of which I handled at a recent Communion Sunday service. The tokens, roughly the size of a 10p coin, bear the initials 'Mr W.F.' (parish minister of the day) and are stamped on the reverse: 'I Cor. 11, 28, 29'. It is amazing to think that the tokens, slightly worn but still completely legible, are used on Gigha to this day.

Another interesting antiquity is the big leaden plate which has a diameter in excess of one foot. This was used as a collection plate in the days when it was not permitted to take money inside a church and the elders had to stand outside to receive churchgoers' contributions. It was then carried round to the vestry before the service commenced.

The Highland Parish Church, in nearby Campbeltown, has a similar plate with holes bored in its base to let rainwater escape.

As with the general history of Gigha, accounts of church life between the 13th and 18th centuries are pretty well mist-shrouded but, although peace and tranquillity now abound in matters ecclesiastical, it was not always so.

The island's earliest religious visitor appears to have been St Cathan, in the 6th century. St Cathan was based on Bute and from there he, as a Columban monk, travelled extensively throughout Kintyre and the isles. He is reputed to have had a cell at Keill, on Gigha, and there is a well in the vicinity which bears his name.

The first church on Gigha was called for St Cathan and later became known as Kilchattan Church. According to the Kintyre Book, the church was built in the 13th century and the ruins of its three-feet thick walls stand surrounded by ancient gravestones just off the sloping road leading to Keill cottages. Forty-feet long by 20 wide, the north wall of the church still supports carvings of Latin and Greek crosses.

The first of two later churches on the same site at Ardminish was built between 1707 and 1712. This was replaced in 1780 and remained Gigha's place of worship until 1923.

The Parish of Gigha and Cara was formed on January 22, 1726, when both islands were officially separated from Killean Parish, on the Kintyre mainland. Unfortunately, no Kirk Session records exist prior to 1791, thanks to their removal by the Rev Dugald MacDougall, who left Gigha and was eventually replaced by the Rev William Fraser. Mr Fraser's induction was made only after the people of Gigha objected most strongly to the appointment, in 1786, by the Duke of Argyll of one Samuel Peat. Their complaint that Peat could not speak Gaelic was upheld by the Presbytery of Kintyre and the Synod of Argyll.

Peat was still protesting to the General Assembly of the Church of Scotland when Mr Fraser entered the pulpit for the first time five years later. However, for some reason, the island populace turned against Mr Fraser and, in 1802 on the advice of the Presbytery of Kintyre, he took his leave.

A total of 15 ministers have held the charge since that time, the longest serving being the Rev James Curdie, MA, who preached for 50 years between 1827 until 1877.

Probably the best-known was the Rev Kenneth MacLeod, DD, the noted Gaelic scholar who served as island minister for 25 years. A great lover of music and poetry it was he who wrote the famous Scots air, 'The Road to the Isles', during the first World War. He sold the copyright for £5 and when the commercial value of the performing rights were pointed out to him he replied: "Living here on lovely Gigha what would I be doing with more money. There's nothing I want. Not a thing."

The recently retired minister, the Rev Herbert Gunneberg, has an interesting curriculum vitae. He was born in 1930 at Duisburg, Germany, and grew up at Rayen Kreis Moers, between the Rhine and the Dutch border, where his father was a schoolteacher. Following his secondary education at Neukirchem he studied for the ministry, variously, at Wupperhal, Mainz, Tubingen and Bonn. On his ordination at Essen in 1962 he was appointed minister of Parish Education there, spending seven years in that post before moving to Glasgow as pastor to the German-speaking church.

45

In 1981 he was affiliated to the Church of Scotland and became minister at Strathfillan, where he preached for nine years prior to his induction on Gigha in 1990. He and wife, Gudrun, a former nurse and social worker, raised six children in Scotland and have had the satisfaction of seeing them all become university graduates.

Prior to the appointment of the popular Rev Bill Bristow to fill the Gigha vacancy, parishioners had, for four months, the pleasure of listening to the Rev Eric Muirhead, a newly-qualified Canadian Presbyterian Church minister. When he was 34-years-old, Eric decided to study for the ministry after having lead a fairly non-ecclesiastical life which saw him, among other things, earn a living as a singer-guitarist in a Country and Western band and as a manager in a tyre factory.

The church manse on Gigha fairly rang with the resonance of Canadian accents during the summer of 1998 when Eric, now 38, and wife Susan, accompanied by their family of Gordon (17), Pamela (15), and twin sons Andrew and Matthew (6), took up residence.

A native of Medicine Hat, Alberta, Eric returned to be ordained in his new parish of Melfort and Tisdale, Saskatchewan, which has a population of around 20,000.

His everlasting memory of life on Gigha, a story perhaps synonymous with most small Scottish islands, concerns the occasion when Eric's car battery ran flat. He was, therefore, forced to accompany Susan on foot to the ferry slipway in order to wave her off on a day trip to mainland Campbeltown and he casually mentioned the battery malfunction to crewman Alasdair McNeill, who also happens to be a church elder and Session Clerk.

On his way home, Eric decided to request the loan of a set of jump leads from Seamus McSporran at the island post office and was flabbergasted to learn that his problem has already been attended to, thanks to the deployment of modern day Gigha jungle drums in the shape of Alasdair's mobile telephone.

The existing Kirk Session records make interesting reading with reports of calumny, immorality and sabbath breaking. Elders were appointed in 1794 in order to prevent such occurrences and the record states:

"The elders will see to it that the people of their several districts go to church. They must examine the conduct of their people on the Lord's Day and use every means to prevent irregularities."

It was the Session's considered judgement that "without due observance of the sabbath there is an end to all religious institutions, all order and reformation. In consequence of the ignorance which unavoidably follows the neglect of religious duties the people will become careless and lax in their morals and the greatest degeneracy and deprivation of matters will ensue."

Between 1769 and 1869 the morning service lasted from 10.30 am until 12.30 pm and the afternoon proceedings had a duration of two hours also, from 2 pm until 4 pm. Everyone was expected to be there.

As in any society, however, laws are made to be broken and Gigha was no exception. The all-powerful Kirk Session met to consider charges against "a great number of people" who had gathered on the beach at Leim on Sunday, February 19, 1786, to await the inevitable coming ashore of a cargo of timber from a shipwreck. The Session contended that the lieges had behaved in a "riotous and indecent fashion" while Divine Service was being held. Fines averaging 2/6d (12¹/₂p) and public reprimands were meted out, all proceeds going to the poor of the island. In addition, John Innes had to pay an extra 10s (50p) for speaking disrespectfully about his elder.

The detested public reprimand, a punishment which meant that miscreants had to sit in a special place in church, was scrapped in 1794 when one of them offered to pay 5s (25p) instead. This was upped to 10s by the elders and the poor gained accordingly.

Another well-documented case concerns the antics of two young ladies called Mary and Maggie. On Sunday, May 4, 1794, Mary called on Maggie at her home in Ardminish bearing a hank of yarn. She asked Maggie to use this 'currency' to obtain a mutchkin of whisky (approximately one pint) from the innkeeper, which she duly did. As the day wore on, more people joined in and more hanks of yarn were surrendered for whisky. In fact, it developed into what is commonly referred to nowadays as a 'session'.

Every participant in the soirée admitted that the event had taken place during Divine Service but it took the Kirk Session so long to interrogate everyone and prepare a cast iron case that no sentence could be passed as Mary had emigrated.

The Session Clerk recorded in 1786: "We deplore the number of cases of calumny which come before us and in future such cases will be very severely dealt with."

Women calling each other a "whore and a liar" seem to have been the most common in that category but there was an interesting case as recently as 1882 when two islanders appeared before the Kirk Session to vehemently deny allegations of grave-robbing against them by a fellow Gigha man.

The two men had been given £2 to buy drink in return for taking on the responsibility of burying several badly disfigured sailors drowned when a boat called the 'Challenge' foundered. They freely admitted to being very drunk when performing their undertaking duties but insisted they wanted it known that they were burying bodies and not raising them. The Session did not condemn the men for being intoxicated and ordered the accuser to apologise publicly in church.

Immorality cases cropped up, too, on a regular basis. The procedure was fairly simple in that a girl appeared before them to name the father of her child. The man would be summoned to present himself and either pay the appropriate fine or deny all knowledge of the affair. In instances of denial, the Session met again several times to hear from witnesses before making a decision on the case. Elders settled many cases in their alloted areas but in the event of an impasse, the matter was brought to the Session's attention.

One such case involved a young lady called Meran, who appeared to her elder to be noticably pregnant, though she denied this and blamed the design of her underwear. A month or two later nature had taken its course and the elder was proved to be correct, whereupon the father named by Meran was fined and reprimanded.

The Session made a puzzling decision in the case of a young unmarried couple whose relationship produced a child. The father of the child was let off, while his uncle, who had permitted them to sleep together in his house, was punished and made to provide for the baby's upbringing.

The undoubted highlight of the year in island church life was the staging of the Sacramental Weekend, a massive communion service which attracted so many visiting ministers and members of their congregations that the population of Gigha trebled. The event, which was always held at the beginning of May, was the culmination of a month's hard work by the minister and elders who visited every home on the island to make sure that disputes were settled and, by asking various biblical questions, to ascertain if individuals were in a fit and ready state to receive communion.

Since the church was too small to accommodate such numbers, a shelter similar in design to a sentry box had to be erected and the 'duty' minister used this while preaching to the hordes of people sitting on the grassy slopes. The wooden hut was quaintly referred to as The Tent.

Visitors began arriving on the Thursday and massed near the church. Many sermons were delivered from The Tent on the Friday and earnest discussions took place between the senior members of the various congregations, but by Saturday an almost carnival atmosphere pervaded. Although many people could be seen reading their bibles or at prayer, others followed more light-hearted pursuits by visiting the inn or strutting around in finery hoping to attract the attention of the opposite sex. Hawkers, tinkers and beggars were also much in evidence.

On Sunday an all-day Communion Service was held in the church, where a long table covered with white linen ran the length of the aisle. Communicants holding the necessary token filed in until the table was full. Visitors were admitted only if they held the appropriate certificates issued by their own parish to say they were prepared for communion. The process was repeated by different ministers throughout the day until all who had sought communion had received it.

Obviously, to cater for such numbers, large quantities of bread and wine were needed and this was carted from Campbeltown to Largie, where a special ferry loaded up and crossed the Gigha Sound.

Changed days, indeed.

Working in Wood

Most 79-year-old grannies or, for that matter, great grannies, are content to sit quietly in a comfortable chair, perhaps knitting for a new arrival or doing a spot of cross stitch, while all of the time reflecting on life gone by.

Not Vie Tulloch. Gigha's famed wood sculptress is still beavering away with a verve that so forcefully belies her years. Well worn cliche it may be, but '79-years-young' describes this fascinating human dynamo perfectly. And her standard wail of:

"I've got *so* much do to," gives a clear idea of her general attitude to life.

Vie was born in Leith in 1920 and, after school, attended Edinburgh Art College. She has a devotion to islands and has lived on the Isle of Man, The Orkneys, Mull, Skye and Gigha. During her early years on Gigha Vie also spent some time as temporary caretaker on Inch Kenneth, off the coast of Mull, where she single-handedly milked cows and took charge of the lambing. She also tended a walled garden attached to the big house.

Inch Kenneth once supported a nunnery and the ghosts of some of the departed sisters are said to frequent the area. The shepherd from Mull who delivered Vie's mail once asked her: "Are you not afraid of the nuns that walk?"

"No, they are women like me."

"Are you not afraid of the Vikings, then?"

"No, I'm three-quarters Shetlander, with a direct line from the Vikings."

"Well, what about the wee folk?"

"No, not the wee folk either."

The shepherd, Archie McFadyen, knew he had met his match and the two became firm friends.

Vie's wood carvings have been shown at one-woman exhibitions in Edinburgh and London, the Royal Scottish Academy and Leeds Art Gallery. She has also undertaken many commissions from both the UK and abroad.

Home, with her dog and a multitude of friendly birds and other wild life, is a neat little shoreside cottage at Gallochoille, which in Gaelic means 'place of the boats'.

She first came to Gigha on family holidays in the mid-fifties with her husband and two children and was enchanted by the environment. Annual sojourns to the island followed, the accommodation being a semi-converted fishing gear store at Rudh a Chinn Mhoir, on the south side of Ardminish Bay, which cost £10 per year.

When her marriage broke up in 1968, Vie decided to settle on Gigha and was offered the cottage in which she now dwells. It was not all plain sailing, though, for the house had lain empty for some time and was so damp that the wallpaper was peeling off the walls. But with typical optimistic energy, the problem was vigorously addressed and soon the cottage and surrounding garden, complete with fish pond, was transformed.

Vie's most pressing problem was how to make a living on Gigha and she tried writing, being no mean scribe, either, but an underlying desire to commit herself to working in wood became too much to resist. The result was the first of her one-woman shows which was followed by a steady flow of commissions.

The islanders were somewhat curious about her at first and Vie remembers sitting on the wooden bench seat on the crowded little open ferry, 'Shuna', with a piece of bog oak in its natural state between her knees. Willie McSporran, my 'Lochranza' shipmate was sitting next to her and he asked what the bit of wood was for. Vie told him she intended to use it to carve a bird and Willie's laconic reply of: "Och, it's no' fit for burning," caused a ripple of laughter on the boat.

She must have impressed Willie with the result, though, because the same man unearthed a large piece of bog oak while ploughing a field at Ardlamy Farm and arranged for its delivery to Gallochoille with farmer Bob Blackwood. This piece of bog oak now represents a minke whale and is fixed to the wall in the reception area of the Gigha Hotel.

Having viewed much of Vie's work over the years I maintain, though my knowledge of the subject is sadly lacking, that this is her masterpiece.

Pleasant weather, of which Gigha gets a good share, sees Vie working barefoot at a special bench set up in her garden.

She chose birds as her theme years ago, when she said: "Birds have suffered more depredation than other living things. They have been very badly hurt by oil pollution and particularly by the insecticide DDT, which has made a great many eggs infertile."

She encourages birdlife into her garden by the copious distribution of breadcrumbs and peanuts and has identified more than 120 species on the island. She also describes herself as a "child of nature who works and worries away in wood" with her assorted tools of mallets, chisels, sandpaper and gouges, shaping it into her earnest appeal for the preservation of life in its completeness.

"Man's first enemy," she says, "is greed, the second is carelessness and the third is lack of courage. How awful if a great grandchild asked me what a butterfly was."

Vie uses hard wood such as cherry, lime or walnut, since they have very little grain and are easier to carve, and prefers the wood to have been felled for 15 to 20 years before use. The finished article is invariably smoothed down and highly polished to portray a silkiness which is a delight to look at and handle.

Vie originally worked in clay but, as she says: "Basically I'm a sculptor. I pare or cut down rather than build up, as you do with clay. I love the feel of wood but working in it is a slow, strenuous process. You can never do many pieces; you have to steal it away. A ripple or a muscle can never be put back once it is cut."

She used dead birds found on the shore as models to sketch and carve and remembers the time she came across a dead shelduck without flesh, but with feathers and skeleton quite complete.

"Now this really was quite a find. I was very lucky. He was picked clean by a peregrine falcon and I must have found him immediately he'd finished. What a fine job he made; eyes, tongue, all the flesh gone and the skeleton and feathers perfect."

Another time, an otter was trapped and drowned in a lobster creel and Vie carried it home to make a detailed study of the animal.

She explains: "I like everything to be perfect and the marvellous thing about wood is that you don't have to send it away to be cast. You are involved in the process from beginning to end. You must know and love your subject. After that you can stylise and throw out a wing in a slightly exaggerated way if you want to. One must not be too hidebound by the design, forgetting the potential in the wood."

Vie Tulloch still has a spring in her step that would do credit to a woman half her age and her fitness at 79 allows her to take part in activities that are only a fond memory to her contemporaries. Recent holidays have seen her clambering among Greek ruins on runs ashore from an Aegean cruise ship, aboard which she spent a delightful three weeks with an 81-year-old friend, climbing in Norway and attending a family wedding in the USA.

Vie also loves sailing and the summer months see her keeping her hand in aboard yachts belonging to acquaintances. She had, at the tender age of 65, a traumatic grounding experience aboard a yacht on South Rona, an island off Skye. She was in 'Nan of Gare', an International eight metre cruiser racer – a strongly built boat of mahogany planking on galvanised steel frames and carrying an exterior lead keel of four tons. She was crewed that day by two grandfathers and a granny (Vie),whose combined ages totalled 210 years and who were taking part in their annual get together cruise.

Vie takes up the story: "South Rona has a sheltered anchorage, but it has a tricky approach and the Clyde Cruising Club directions were being followed, we thought, to the letter.

"As we made into Acarsaid Mor, South Rona, the tide had just began to ebb. It was almost 1600 hours and completely windless. We were moving slowly, but so near the grey and pink granite that I felt the back of my neck prickling.

"The tiller lifted under my hand. We're touching, I whispered. No. But we were. The water was so clear, the rock and seaweed were there under us on the port side, and deep black water to starboard. Seconds separated the quietness of the navigator's voice and the hectic unlashing of the spinnaker poles and jamming them into any rock crevice and heaving on them to push us off. We thought she was free for a moment, but it was wishful thinking.

"It was the most lonely, empty, uninhabited place, and the tide was going fast. Nan was beginning to cowp and we had to get fenders under her. We made every move about the yacht with great care, like cats, for fear we would upset the precarious balance as the water crept away, exposing the pinkish rock."

Shortly afterwards, a yacht with two Americans aboard arrived on the scene and more fenders, lines and anchors were rigged to hold the 'Nan of Gare', which by this time had heeled crazily.

Granny Vie, as the bantamweight, was appointed salvor of foodstuffs and beverages from below decks.

"It took enormous effort to pull the heavy mahogany drawers upwards against gravity without making too much movement in the struggle. How dry the mouth gets when you are hardly daring to breathe in case a false move might send your boat nosediving down the rocks."

Vie says that she "pondered and prayed" aboard the American's yacht until 3am, when it was time to prepare for high water shortly afterwards. The early June dawn revealed the 'Nan of Gare' almost afloat and, minutes later, thanks to concentrated prayer, the boat literally leapt into the air and slid off keel first into the water.

This incident did not dull Vie's appetite for adventure in any way and she was soon back on the high seas. A remarkable lady, indeed, and one wonders just what she is going to get up to next.

A True Islander

One of Gigha's most endearing and, indeed, enduring characters is 81-years-old Angus MacAlister, a man who has lived the life of a Scottish islander in the true sense of the word.

Angus, whom I have mentioned earlier, still goes to sea to tend crab and lobster creels, this despite the fact that a major heart operation he underwent a few years ago would have caused many other men to forego such pursuits. Transport to and from the South Pier from his home at Gigalum Cottages is a vintage bicycle, the age of which is anyone's guess.

Naturally, I have had many, many yarns with Angus and the day I visited him to discuss this book was one of bright sunshine, but with a brisk, cold easterly wind blowing. Perfect conditions to round off the curing process of three big lythe (pollack) which were pinned to his washing line. Angus buries fish such as lythe or saithe in salt for a week and then, weather permitting, hangs them to drain and dry for a further four days. The fish, by then rock hard, are put into a dry flour bag and kept in an airing cupboard for anything up to a year.

"You've never tasted the likes o' them, along with some good mashed potatoes," he told me as a bag containing about eight dried salted lythe, hard as teak, was produced from a cupboard in the cottage.

The sight of the fish reminded me of the time I had enjoyed a successful sea angling excursion and I telephoned Angus on my return to inquire if he would like a pair of bonnie big lythe. The answer was obviously in the affirmative so I carefully skinned and filleted the fish and delivered them to Gigalum. However, I received a scolding for having had the audacity to bone them!

"Never fillet lythe. The nearer the bone, the tastier they are. Always remember that," I was instructed.

Angus's home is equipped with the usual modern conveniences but he speaks fondly about his life on Gigha of not so very long ago, when things were a bit different.

"We lived off the sea and the land. There were no such things as deep freezers or fridges or washing machines."

He has nostalgic memories of one of his favourite dishes, casseroled cormorant, or skart as the species is probably better known in Scotland. The seabirds were left to hang for three days before skinning and cooking.

"I'm telling ye, if I put a plateful of skart in front of ye, I'll bet ye would think ye were eatin' steak," Angus told me.

Butcher meat was available at the island shop once per week or was bought in limited quantities on occasional trips to the mainland as it had to be eaten within a day or two of purchase.

Porridge, fish and seafood of all kinds, potatoes and plenty of fresh home-grown vegetables featured strongly on Angus's menu. Mutton flank or ham ends were generally available to make the stock for delicious broth or potato soup. Eggs from his hens and ducks were used in baking and eaten also. To this day he draws fresh water from a spring close to his house rather than use the mains supply.

Angus was fiercely independent and industrious as far as providing for his wife and family was concerned. In the winter months he was the island's fencing and draining contractor, and all the farmers were grateful for his expertise on such matters. This was the time, too, for gathering periwinkles from the shore.

To supplement his agricultural income he began fishing for lobsters, originally in a 14-foot rowing boat, and has continued to do so ever since, between March and September. All his lobster pots were hand made in the big shed alongside his house.

Another important source of income to Angus was as stevedore aboard the many puffers and coasters which called at Gigha in the days before the roll-on, roll-off ferry. Back in the 1950's he was usually part of a three-man team employed to discharge cargoes consisting of lime, road metal, bricks, coal, road chips, timber or gravel. The going rate at that time was 3s 6d (17p) per ton, which was split three ways.

Emptying the 120-ton capacity puffers was back-breaking work. Angus recalls: "It was a long day and very hard work. There were no cranes or grabs so it was all shovellin'.

"I've seen us startin' at four o'clock in the mornin' and carryin' on till six at night.

"Whiles, if the skipper was keen to get away we would work on till nine at night. They would let go their ropes the minute the last shovelful was oot and get under way before even the hatches were back on."

The various cargoes were distributed throughout the island by Neil Bannatyne, who operated Bedford tipper lorries which were craned on to Gigha's South Pier from the MV 'Lochiel'.

The last cargo Angus worked on was aboard the MV 'Polarlight', which, along with the MV 'Glen Etive', carried the building materials to Gigha for use in the extensive refurbishment of the island hotel in 1977. Two days discharging of the 300-ton cargo netted Angus and the two other stevedores 37p per ton between them.

He also made occasional trips on puffers to various west coast ports if there was a shortage of crew.

He well remembers the names of the boats, which sailed under the company flags of Ross and Marshall, Hay, Gardner and Hamilton. 'Warlight', 'Starlight', 'Moonlight', 'Stormlight', 'Limelight', 'Lady Isle', 'Lady Morvern', 'Halcyon', 'Glen Rosa', 'Glen Cloy', 'Spartan', 'Kaffir', 'Pibroch'. They all roll off his tongue easily.

Does Angus hanker for the days gone by?

"Well, yes and no. But there was something special about Gigha in the fifties and sixties. Things certainly weren't all that bad".

Community Chest

As the autumn leaves begin to fall and the tourist season is but a memory, Mrs Lena McGeachy, of Burnside, Gigha, performs a little personal ritual which has become an annual occurrence – the presentation of a much appreciated sum of money to the island church.

The raising of this cash for church funds, which so amply personifies Lena's continual allegiance to the community, is the result of the sale of home produce and crafts at a small summer wayside stall set up on a table outside her home. An average of £200 is presented each year to Gigha Parish Church.

Items on sale include home-made jams and jellies, crocheted bookmarks, knitted car novelties and socks, each with a specific price tag. A 'donation' is asked in return for second hand books on display.

The tiny stall was first set up about 16 years ago and, although it is always unattended, Lena relies on the honesty of visitors to Gigha when it comes to paying for any items taken. The old syrup tin 'cash box' has only been interfered with once, though this is surely akin to rifling a church offering box and is a somewhat sad indictment on modern society.

Lena's activities are part of an overall community spirit on Gigha which, I am glad to say, is still prevalent. Genuine concern, not borne out of nosiness, is shown if someone falls ill or is otherwise troubled and help is given when possible.

Locals take part in various activities and social gatherings and the occasional wedding is a guaranteed 'open house' in the true tradition of the Scottish islander's way of life.

Whist drives, carpet bowls and badminton evenings help to take some of the dreariness out of the long winter and sales of work in aid of school, village hall or church funds are always well-supported.

Summer evenings often see impromptu fishing trips being organised aboard any one of the considerable number of small boats owned on Gigha and the spoils are always shared equally.

Music at the village hall dances is usually provided by the recently re-formed Gigha Band, a trio of 'golden oldies' whose combined ages total in excess of 200 years. The band members, Graham McCulloch (accordion), Ian Wilkieson (drums), and Malcolm Allan (keyboards), first played together more than 40 years ago. Graham had just been demobbed from the RAF, during which time he had practised regularly on the 'box', and the meeting place was a shed at the back of his house. In the early days Ian used a biscuit tin as a drum and Malcolm played piano accordion.

After about a year of honing their musical skills the Gigha Band felt confident enough to face the public and began to play at occasional dances and weddings. As the years passed, however, the band gradually split up and it was not until all three had attained retirement age that the decision to get together again was taken, performing under the title of 'The Resurrected Three.' On the evening of their debut in the hall, the MC could not for the life of him remember the band's new name and caused an explosion of laughter when he announced that 'The Three Erections' were ready to take the stage!

The island's health and welfare is looked after admirably by district nurse Mrs Margaret Wilkieson, a real angel of mercy who replaced Sister Dorothy Wilkieson, her mother-in-law, in that capacity in the autum of 1997. Mrs Wilkieson snr served the island for 28 years and the esteem in which she was held was marked by presentations to her at a surprise social function in the Gigha Hotel. Included in her retirement gifts was a token of appreciation from the Clyde Fishermen's Association for the sterling assistance given by her to injured or sick trawlermen who used Gigha as a base over the years.

Already an RGN, Margaret's appointment as Gigha's district nurse and midwife was just reward for the effort she put in during a lengthy period of study at Glasgow's Caledonian University and, practically, doing the rounds in the Campbeltown area.

Margaret kept her car at Tayinloan and, for 30 weeks, crossed the Gigha Sound by fishing boat at 5.30am each Monday and Tuesday, her university days. She returned to the island at night, again by trawler, following a 230-mile round trip by road. It was with delight that islanders learned that Margaret had been awarded a B.Sc in Health Studies at the end of it all.

Dr N J Gourlay, of the Muasdale GP practice across the water in Kintyre, holds a weekly surgery on Gigha, but is also available for consultation at his base should the need arise.

Gigha's political and environmental interests come under the auspices of a seven-strong Community Council, headed by chairman Willie McSporran. The council meets every three months in the village hall to discuss business pertaining to the general good of the community and representations or suggestions are submitted to the parent Argyll and Bute Council at Lochgilphead for further debate.

Despite many station closures around the UK coast, the Gigha Auxiliary Coastguard unit is still very much to the fore. The Auxiliary-in-Charge, John Martin, controls a six-man team from a fully equipped base in the top floor of a former bistro called, appropriately enough, 'The Boathouse,' on the shores of Ardminish Bay.

The building, formerly known as 'The Storehouse,' was used for that purpose when small cargo vessels called with all manner of things in their holds. The top floor area, is kept in immaculate order by the auxiliaries and still has an operational hatch/ doorway, where goods were taken in after being hoisted from ground level by block and tackle set up on a special gantry. John, who has served as an auxiliary coastguard for 25 years and is the holder of a long service medal, has been called out on many occasions to assist vessels and people in difficulty. His most poignant moment came, however, in 1991 with the grounding and eventual total loss of the Russian klondyker, 'Kartli,' from which the bodies of two dead seamen still on board had to be removed.

"It was quite an emotional time for all concerned," said John.

Another mishap which he has vivid memories of was the helicopter rescue of an elderly yachting couple during a south-easterly gale. He remembers well the name of the yacht, 'Iskra', and its occupants, Frank and Wendy.

The 'Iskra' moored in Ardminish Bay but began dragging its anchor as the wind suddenly increased in fury. A Mayday call for assistance was put out by Frank when he realised he was powerless to stop the drift and a Sea King helicopter was scrambled from Prestwick.

John tells how the couple were actually airlifted before the yacht grounded on the beach. They were landed on Gigha, safe, but both suffering from hypothermia and, as John puts it, "perishing with cold."

The 'Iskra' was later successfully refloated.

Fortunately, many years have passed since there was a major fire on Gigha but the island retains a volunteer fire-fighting force of seven people. Regular drills are carried out throughout the year, supervised by a full-time fire officer from the mainland. At the time of writing, the Gigha fire volunteers have a minimum of equipment which is stored in a hut beside the shop. Their role is one of 'fire containing' until outside help arrives. This is set to change, though, by the construction of a new fire house and the provision of a small fire engine, which will enable the Gigha contingent to tackle blazes with confidence.

Hotel and Leisure

Like most small Scottish islands, Gigha's focal point is the hotel, an establishment which has stood on the same site since its construction in the 1700's.

The tenancy of the Gigha Hotel for many years included the adjacent South Ardminish Farm and this arrangement remained in force until as recently as 1966. In that year, Ken Roebuck and his wife, Eila, took over the hotel from the last hotelier/farmer, Donald Allan, who continued farming and had a new bungalow built alongside the hotel. He remained there until the 1980's, farming both North and South Ardminish, before moving to the mainland. The farm buildings have since been converted for use as stores and workshops.

The hotel is now managed by island director William Howden, who splits his time between this and the running of other estate affairs.

In years gone by, apparently, the innkeeper slept in an adjoining hayloft when the four rooms of the hotel were let during the summer months. Extensive renovations carried out during 1976/77 saw the hayloft and cattle byre being demolished to make way for a dining room and nine first floor bedrooms which were erected on the site. A manager's flat was also incorporated within the building.

When Malcolm Potier took over the island, the manager was rehoused and the self-contained flat turned into an additional four en-suite rooms.

Further expansion of the Gigha Hotel took place in 1997, when an extensive guest lounge was added. This tastefully decorated and furnished room has proved to be a valued addition, both for its comfort and the wonderful views from its windows of the Sound of Gigha. The bedrooms were substantially upgraded and the reception area enlarged, also, as part of the refurbishment.

A total of eight local staff, some seasonal, are joined each year by temporary employees such as barmen, kitchen porters and waitresses – most of them from an agency which specialises in finding employment for young South Africans and New Zealanders who are 'doing the world tour'. Many a visitor has been puzzled by the sound of a cheery greeting of: "G'd die to yuh cobber. What kin ah git yuh?"

There has always been a bar in the hotel and many a yarn, tall or true, has been spun over the years, no doubt stimulated by the effects of a few glasses of 'Uisge Beatha'. Hotel residents, locals and yachstmen – ashore for the evening from the popular Ardminish Bay anchorage – create a real cosmopolitan atmosphere and numerous lasting friendships have had their origins in the snug public bar of the Gigha Hotel.

As in any pub anywhere, special 'characters' can be found who go out of their way to make holidaymakers or daytrippers welcome. No visit to the Gigha Hotel bar would be complete without having a chat with Calum McNeill and his friend, Katie Connely, for the furtherance of one's education!

A fair number of hotel guests actually fly in to Gigha by private aeroplane. Usually pilot/owners, they make use of the airstrip at the south end of the island which was made up by Malcolm Potier during his time as laird. He used it to land his own light aircraft and saw it as a necessary facility in his efforts to attract businessmen to conferences in Achamore House.

The grass strip is 720 metres long, with a breadth of 40 metres, and is capable of landing a twin-engined aeroplane. Gigha is a convenient 30 minutes flying time from Glasgow and members of various flying clubs use the island airstrip frequently. It has also become a favourite setting-down place of the North of Scotland Microlight Club, and up to 15 of the little flying machines can sometimes be seen buzzing around above Gigha. Landing charges are reasonable at £15 per single-engined aeroplane and £10 for a microlight.

Golf was introduced on Gigha in the late 1800's and continued to be played at the Leim course until around 1925. There followed a 60-year gap until 1986, when keen local golfers Alastair 'Plumber' Brown and gamekeeper John Wight designed and built a nine-hole course at Tarbert Farm. In 1988, estate plans were laid to form a golf course at Drumeonbeg Farm and Alastair and John, again, were responsible for the lay-out and creation of the new course.

The first ball was driven off only two months after work started and Alastair has continued in his role as greenkeeper to the present day. A flock of sheep is turned on to the course during the winter months as an effective method of keeping the grass down.

The friendly little nine-hole course is gaining in popularity with hotel guests, other visitors to the island and mainland golf club members who often have 'a round across the Sound'.

Gigha Golf Club is now affiliated to the Scottish Golf Union, which means that, on production of three score cards, members are issued with an official handicap and are eligible to take part in competitions anywhere. In fact, Mrs Sandra Howden has competed successfully in several tourneys, returning to Gigha with silverware.

Seamus McSporran and wife, Margaret, have run Gigha's shop and Post Office for over 30 years

The scene of many a happy holiday, Gigha Hotel taken from the Ferry Crofts

A proud moment for Seamus McSporran in Duart Castle, on Mull, as he receives his BEM from Lord MacLean, Lord Lieutenant of Argyll

The first motorised vehicle ever to be landed on Cara. This tractor was ferried across to the island on board MFV Speedwell on Christmas Eve, 1973

Vie Tulloch, Gigha's renowned sculptress

Jimmy and Olive Robinson, who have farmed both Drumeonbeg and Achamore

Angus MacAlister, of Gigalum, who, at 80 years of age, still maintains a very active lifestyle

Miss Betty MacNeill, of Keill, is a mine of information on Gigha in bygone days

The 'Loch' class ferry 'Lochranza' docks at the slipway in Ardminish Bay

'Lochranza' leaves behind a picturesque scene at Ministers Pier

Island director William Howden with wife Sandra, son Alastair and baby daugher Alison

The remains of the old mill, on the west side, where corn was threshed many years ago. The building in the forefront is fully maintained as a holiday cottage

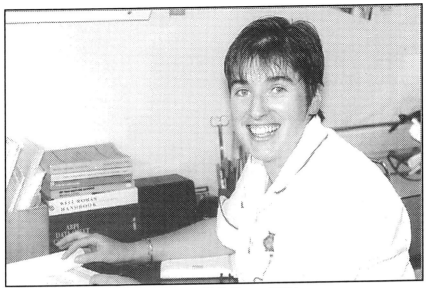

Gigha's angel of mercy, District Nurse and midwife Margaret Wilkieson

On the bridge of 'Bruernish' on her first run from the new slipway are (l to r): Councillor O'Halloran, skipper James Robertson and the ferry's new master, Iain McKechnie, of Gigha

L to R (top) Lachie Wotherspoon, John Bannatyne, Johnnie Andrew and Freddy Gillies

Harry on Cara

Harry Teggin is a clever man, having spent a long time in architecture and town planning. He is also a rational man and an easy conversationalist whose perceptive opinions on most things are valid and, indeed, welcome.

He lives for much of the time on Gigha's satellite island, Cara, reputed to be haunted by a Brownie, a benevolent elf, and Harry believes in its presence with utter conviction, so much so that he refers to 'it' as Angus.

Cara lies about three-quarters of a mile south of Gigha and is one mile long by half a mile broad. It is a pleasant little green island, treeless and with several attractive sandy bays. Goats roam freely and Cara supports a thriving rabbit colony but Harry, and as often as possible his family, are the only other residents though at one time the island had a population of 22.

Stories detailing the Brownie's activities on Cara originated many years ago and have been immortalised locally. The Brownie is said to be the ghost of a Macdonald, owners of Cara for centuries, who was slain by a Campbell. Legend has it that the attic room in the laird's home – Harry's Cara House – is the Brownie's headquarters.

The impish humorous behaviour of the Brownie has even been catalogued in several serious literary works relating to Gigha and surroundings. In his knowledgable publication of 1939 entitled 'The Antiquities of Gigha', the Rev R S G Anderson devoted a chapter to Cara and, in particular, to the Brownie. He wrote: "The Brownie's tragic origin had evidently not injured its sense of humour, which was most frequently, like that of its race, of an impish kind. One story tells of two men, sent by the Laird of Largie, the owner, to fetch over a cask of wine from the big cellar under the kitchen of Cara House. They had evidently no idea of the dignity or the omniscience of a Brownie, for they spoke of it with levity. The gangplank was laid down from the entry into the cellar, but when they tried to roll the barrel up, it was immovable. Do as they would, it stayed put. In the end they were driven to make humble apologies to the creature they had offended, praying that it would not get them into trouble with their master. Thereupon in a moment the barrel ran up the plank itself, out the door, rolled helter-skelter to the sea, clearing banks and bounding over rocks, and never stopped until it reached the place where the boat was moored to the shore."

Rev Anderson also tells the story of a travelling tailor who made derisory remarks in the house about the very idea of a Brownie. Shortly afterwards the tailor had to cross in darkness to the kitchen, " but as soon as he stepped out of the window light he received a buffet on the jaw that thoroughly drove out all scepticism."

Mrs Lena McGeachy, a Gigha woman now in her seventies, told me a convincing story that involved the Brownie and her grandfather.

This man, George Allan, and his son, Malcolm, were rowing to Cara's south end to haul their lobster creels. It was a hot day and George felt thirsty so they pulled the boat to the shore in the vicinity of a good fresh water spring. They got out of the boat and, as her grandfather drank his fill, Malcolm had a look at a seabird's nest of eggs. Back in the boat, Malcolm began rowing but was puzzled by the disappearance of his footspar, a piece of wood in the bottom of the boat designed to stop his feet sliding as he handled the oars. His father knew nothing of the footspar and said it must have been left on Gigha before setting out, but Malcolm was adamant that he had been using it on their way to Cara. A fruitless search of the immediate shoreline ensued and the men continued on their way.

The following day, as they passed the same place, Malcolm told his father to look up at a nook in the rockface, many yards from where they had gone ashore, for, jammed into this niche, was the missing footspar. Cara was completely uninhabited when this took place.

Another weird Brownie incident which has occurred in living memory was experienced by Angus McGougan, the last man to work a croft on Cara. Angus had that day, with his family, crossed to Gigha for supplies at the island shop. However, a sudden storm blew up and they were unable to make the return crossing in their small boat. On returning to Cara the following day Angus went immediately to the byre to milk the few cows he had left tethered there and was astonished to discover that the milking had been done and the cows turned out to pasture. Again, there was not another living soul on Cara at that time.

'Lochranza' shipmate, Alasdair, told me of a visit he made to Cara about 16 years ago with the late Angus McNeill, affectionately known as 'the wee man'. Angus at one time farmed Kinererach and was another Gigha man with whom I had many a yarn.

Alasdair and Angus, in the former's boat, went to the island to collect some fence posts from a dismantled sheep pen which were to be re-used on Gigha. Alasdair remembers vividly that Angus would not get out of the boat until he had solemnly doffed his cap and wished the Brownie a profoundly reverent "good morning."

This could possibly have stemmed from a previous incident when Angus, along with Alec Bickett, of Leim Farm, agreed to assist Achamore Farm's John MacDonald in the round-up of a flock of sheep on Cara. For some unknown reason, the two well-trained sheepdogs brought to carry out the task began whining and stubbornly refused to work or obey commands. Minutes later the animals leapt into the sea, swam away from the island and were eventually rescued on the point of exhaustion.

Though he is based in Glasgow, Harry crosses to Cara as often as he can. He first saw the island and its ruined house 27 years ago when he was involved with the Landmark Trust in seeking out appropriately aged or romantically-strong places in need of renovation. His plans met with the approval of Cara's proprietor at the time, John Macdonald, of Largie.

For some reason, however, the Landmark Trust lost interest but Harry was determined to do something with Cara. Tentative inquiries about the possible purchase of the island were met with a polite refusal, the laird pointing out that the Macdonald line was dependant on a continuing identification with and allegiance to Cara, a situation similar to the ravens in the Tower of London or the apes on the Rock of Gibraltar. He was, though, offered the next best thing – a perpetuity feu at an annual rent of one penny!

Macdonald agreed to sell Harry the derelict Cara House, the

only dwelling on the island. Built in 1730, the house was in a sorry state, rat infested and full of guano thanks to years of occupation by rock doves.

Over the next eight years Harry transformed Cara House into the comfortable dwelling it is today. To do this he used 14 tons of timber, six tons of slates, and 34 windows. He has his own generator for electricity and for pumping the domestic water supply from a well through a filtration unit. The house is lit by both gas and electricity and has its own sewage system. Accommodation consists of five bedrooms, two bathrooms, dining room, kitchen/larder, living room, workroom, engineroom and cellar, where he used to keep a still. The Brownie, or Angus, now resides in a closet under the stair.

It was while renovating Cara House that Harry struck up a wonderful rapport with the islanders of Gigha, in particular Graham McCulloch and Ian Wilkieson, the fishermen who transported so much of the raw materials to Cara on the MFV 'Speedwell'.

Caledonian MacBrayne played its part, too, and the Island class ferry 'Canna' actually landed a five-ton truck loaded with furniture and a tractor on Cara. Harry had heard that the boat was due for a refit in a Clydeside shipyard and more or less 'hitched a lift' from the Oban area. The company was pleased to be involved in the scheme and charged a token £72 for the service.

Harry, nobly assisted by Argyll and Bute's MP, Ray Michie, won a notable battle with the authorities over the charging of poll tax in respect of Cara House. They pointed out there was no street lighting, uplifting of refuse, water mains, telephone, gas or electricity mains, roadways and a host of other things. In fact, all the basic amenities had been provided by Harry himself.

When Harry talks about 'Angus' it is difficult for the listener to question the credibility of the situation. He says a strange, though by no means uncomfortable, feeling envelopes him as soon as he sets foot on Cara.

"It's something far beyond myself," he says.

When I spoke to Harry he had just spent four days on his own in Cara House and did not feel at all lonely. Angus tells him to do things, like checking the boat's moorings. Sure enough, on such occasions he has found shackles on the verge of parting or knots loosened.

Another time Harry and his sons decided to spend some time exploring on Cara. The weather was brisk, to say the least, so before leaving the house they laid a fire in the hearth ready to be lit on their return. Two hours later they came back to find a welcoming fire blazing merrily, having obviously been ignited only minutes before they entered the house.

On another occasion, Angus persuaded Harry it was time to look at the immobile Massey Ferguson tractor, which had lain unused for more than three years. He was convinced that the steering on the machine was seized, thus rendering it inoperable and he was about to begin stripping down work when, completely out of the blue, a man wandered towards him. He explained that he had come ashore from his yacht and would like permission to look around the island. As he talked, the man's eyes seldom strayed from the tractor and Harry explained that he thought the machine's steering was stuck.

"It's not the steering, it's the kingpins," said the stranger. Who was he? None other than the managing director of Massey Ferguson Ltd.

"Why," asks Harry, "on the very day that Angus told me to look at the tractor after more than three years did this man, of all people, arrive on Cara? It's all so wonderfully weird."

An incident with much more serious overtones almost led to Harry being prosecuted by Strathclyde Police a few years ago. He posesses, quite legally, a rifle, but his former 'gun cupboard' was underneath his son's mattress. He was quite horrified to discover one day that the rifle had disappeared and it failed to turn up after an extensive search.

Take the proper course of action, thought Harry, and the matter was duly reported to the police in Campbeltown, whereupon a CID officer was sent to the scene. Routine questioning uncovered the fact that the door of Cara House is never locked and, even worse, that Harry did not have a lockfast gun cupboard; a matter which, in the eyes of the law, is of some gravity. He was, consequently, cautioned and warned of the possibility of prosecution.

Some days later, for some further inexplicable reason, Harry decided to move his wine supply from Angus's closet beneath the stairs to a first floor room and the missing firearm was discovered stashed behind some boxes.

The then Chief Constable of Strathclyde, Patrick Hamill, let

Harry off with a stern warning to keep the rifle under lock and key in future, but could not resist asking in his official letter: "So, Angus has been at it again, has he?"

I have asked lots of level-headed people on Gigha who have crossed to Cara over the years for their opinions on the Brownie and the consensus is a resounding agreement that there is 'something' there.

I stepped ashore on the magical isle for the first time a few months ago and, yes, I removed my baseball cap with a flourish before I got out of the boat!

A Man of Many Hats

I was standing at the bar, of an evening, in the lounge of the Paris Hotel, Polcoverack, a tiny Cornish fishing village near Land's End, and happened to mention that I lived on the Isle of Gigha. Never for a moment did I imagine that anyone within earshot would have a clue as to Gigha's whereabouts, but a gravelly West Country voice from a few yards distant inquired: "And 'ow is Seamus keepin', then?"

Slightly taken aback I may have been that someone in that far-off seaside hamlet knew of the island but I was not in the least surprised that the gent had asked after Seamus McSporran, whose name is as synonymous with Gigha as whisky is with Scotland.

The Cornishman, it transpired, had been on a walking holiday in Scotland and had spent a night on Gigha as a bed and breakfast client of Seamus. The hospitality and food, he said, were tremendous and only a tightly prepared advance schedule forced the man from remaining on the island for a longer period.

"But oi'll be back, oi'll be bound, he said.

Seamus is a prodigious character who, along with his wife, Margaret, has run the island shop/post office and guest house for the past 33 years... among other things! For Seamus, perhaps better described as 'Mr Gigha', has an astonishing work load which entitles him to wear no less than 12 hats. It was actually 14, until 1993, when he was forced to hang up his auxiliary fire chief's helmet on attaining the service's obligatory retirement age. He also retired as special constable in 1998.

At present, Seamus serves Gigha in the following capacities: sub-postmaster, postman, petrol pump attendant, shopkeeper, undertaker, taxi-operator, council rent collector, insurance agent, piermaster, guest house keeper, registrar, ambulance driver.

If all the words written about this quite extraordinary man in the many newspaper and magazine articles he has featured in were collated in one volume, many hours of reading would be required to digest the information.

Seamus's day begins at 7am, when he rises to prepare breakfast for overnight guests. He is usually to be seen on the 0830 ferry to Tayinloan, where newspapers, mail, bread and provisions are loaded into the familiar blue van in preparation for the return sailing. Most of the mail is sorted on the trip across and, when the van is unloaded on Gigha, it is time to set off round the island on his moped to deliver the letters. Obviously, the shop has to be looked after while Seamus is on the road and this duty falls upon Margaret, ably assisted by Mrs Margaret Andrew, who has worked with the McSporrans for many years.

In all the time that Seamus served as Gigha's special constable, he was never actually called out in his official capacity.

"Gigha is a very quiet, law-abiding island. Just the way I like it," he says.

"I never, ever had to make an arrest in my 24 years in the job."

Hopefully, his successor, Alasdair McNeill, will enjoy a similar crime free term of office.

When he was appointed rent collector for the old Argyll County Council, Seamus was asked what he considered an appropriate honorarium would be.

He told me: "At that time, the road fund tax on my car was just about due for renewal so I suggested to the council that the equivalent value of the licence on an annual basis would be a suitable remuneration. I think the excise duty on a motor car then was about £25."

Countless motoring miles have been completed since that time and the price of a road fund licence has spiralled considerably but Seamus, uncomplainingly, still receives his original annual fee.

His remarkable life began 60 years ago in Brae House, a somewhat grandly named trim little cottage which stands on the hillside overlooking Ardminish village and the Sound of Gigha. His was a Gaelic-speaking household and Seamus could not speak a word of English until he was enrolled in the island school at the age of five.

"It means I can swear in both languages," he says with

typical humour.

When he left school at 15, Seamus joined the late Angus Wilkieson as his assistant in the Gigha shop and post office. Apart from two years spent on national service in the RAF he has been there ever since, taking over as boss in 1965.

Telephones were rare on Gigha in those days but the instrument was a necessary piece of equipment for use in business of an official nature which cropped up occasionally. The post office telephone, therefore, was a vital communications link and, by natural progression, Seamus fell heir to most of the positions.

He met his future wife, Margaret, on Gigha when she was on holiday from her native Preston, Lancashire and romance blossomed. They have a son, Alastair, and a daughter, Margaret, both of whom have successfully pursued careers on the mainland.

Along the way, Seamus has collected three long service medals and, probably his proudest possession, the British Empire Medal for services to the Gigha community. The award was presented to him by the late Lord Maclean of Duart and Morvern (Lord Lieutenant of Argyll) at a ceremony in Duart Castle, on the Island of Mull, in 1989.

Another keepsake Seamus has cherished is a warm letter of thanks he received in the same year from Earl Spencer, brother of the late Princess Diana.

The then Viscount Althorp was in charge of an NBC Television news team which filmed extensively on Gigha when an American actress expressed interest in buying the island.

In his letter, Viscount Althorp described how the newscast had been aired across the United States and he thanked Seamus profusely for his co-operation, describing him as the film's "star of the show."

Most people on Gigha, myself included, have had cause to be grateful to Seamus McSporran for some reason or other and his often-used pronouncement of "it's no bother" is one that is spoken with sincerity.

Island Craftsmen

Scottish islands have something of a reputation when it comes to producing individuals who possess marvellous practical skills, and Gigha is no exception. Graham McCulloch, of Woodend, and Angus McVean, of Ardminish (Gigha's oldest resident at the age of 85), are both eminently talented craftsmen in wood, though they pursue different methods of expression.

Graham channels his carpentry energies into boatbuilding and repairing while Angus prefers to create wooden pieces of a more delicate nature – violins.

Graham's latest venture, the complete renovation of a semi-derelict 14-foot clinker built dinghy, has drawn many admiring looks and favourable comment though he admits he would rather have built the boat from scratch, as he reckons it would have been easier.

Graham is also an accomplished engineer and is yet another islander who goes about life with a vigour that makes a mockery of his 69 years. His appetite for engineering was whetted by the completion of two years national service as a mechanic in the RAF, a period in his life he enjoyed immensely.

"This valuable training was free and I made the most of it. I was very grateful to be given the chance," he says.

Enginering runs in this amiable bachelor's family and his uncles were, respectively, a Royal Naval chief engineer and a garage proprietor.

Boatbuilding, however, is his first love and he talks easily on the subject. "I was always fascinated by the way a boat was built and I used to love watching the old Gigha carpenters at work.

"I would also study old wrecks closely to see how they were constructed and note all the details.

"Building and renovating boats as a hobby is just something that is in me that wants to come out. I suppose you could say I'm daft about boats."

Graham worked on the small open wooden ferries which plied the Sound of Gigha until, in 1956, he bought the MFV 'Speedwell' (CN 104). There followed 23 years of scallop dredging and lobster potting until 1979, when he joined Caledonian MacBrayne's 'Island' class 'Bruernish', the car ferry which had been introduced to the Gigha route. Attendance at Glasgow and Leith Nautical Colleges saw him emerge successfully with an engineering ticket and both radar and firefighting proficiency certificates. Graham eventually became skipper of the 'Bruernish'.

Throughout his career with Caledonian MacBrayne he carried on his favourite leisure-time activity and began the extensive refurbishment of the former Gigha ferry, 'Jamie Boy'. The 22-feet-long boat, which was built by the Jones yard in Buckie in 1949, had lain abandoned at Killean, near Tayinloan, for some time before Graham had it transported to Gigha and into the big shed at the rear of his house. It was here that he fitted a Kelvin P4 20hp engine but the hull was pulled outside for completion of the masterful carpentry work that was carried out on the boat.

The first job was to draw sample nails from different sections of the planking and Graham was satisfied to note that their condition was still good. He then strengthened the hull by fitting extra frames and installed new flooring. An eye-pleasing fully-fitted deckhouse and galley, complete with steering cockpit and masts were added to give the former ferry a truly cabin cruiser look.

The 'Jamie Boy' is launched religiously each spring and can be seen bobbing at her moorings at the Minister's Pier, near the ferry slipway, until late autumn, when she is taken ashore for the winter.

When the 'Jamie Boy' is afloat, Graham makes an annual passage to Rathlin Island, off the Antrim coast of Northern Ireland, where he has many friends. The boat is also used for other island visits and occasional diving excursions.

Angus McVean was born in one of the Drumeonbeg Crofts in 1914 and spoke nothing but Gaelic until he went to school at the age of five, where he learned English.

His family worked Highfield Farm for 30 years and it was

there that Angus first took an interest in violin music, learning to play the instrument in his twenties.

When he left Highfield Angus joined the crew of the small ferry, 'Jamie Boy', but, surprisingly for an islander who loved lobster fishing, he did not enjoy life as a ferryman and returned to farming at South Ardminish three years later. It was around this time that Angus decided to have a go at making a violin from scratch and he made contact with a Birmingham company, Sidney Evans Ltd., who supplied him with the necessary materials and strings. The result was a beautifully-crafted musical instrument – the first of a line of violins.

Angus showed me round the big garden shed in which his musical creations are patiently fashioned, and I was fascinated by an array of violin body moulds, tuning screws, finger boards, strings and the home-made tools he uses. He explained how the top and bottom pieces of the body, usually pine and sycamore respectively, are joined together by a narrow strip of fine veneer shaped by a hot iron and he showed me the method of fixing the finger board. Several coats of an exceedingly fine varnish are applied to give a lustrous appearance to the finished article.

Angus's violins have found homes with grateful owners far and wide, including the United States of America. In all, he has made "more than a dozen" and when I told him I thought it was a pity he had waited so long before taking up the hobby, he replied: "Aye, you are right. I left it far too late in life."

Angus's last few years of working life were spent in the gardens at Achamore House, a job he enjoyed doing immensely. He still has the punt – now nearly 100 years old – that he used for lobster and mackerel fishing, a pursuit he followed until recently.

The School Years

October 18, 1997, was an important date in the history of education on Gigha. For on that day Gigha Primary School celebrated its 100th birthday. The centenary was marked by an exhibition in the schoolrooms, with pupils dressed in Victorian style, and the staging of social events on the island.

It is easy to imagine the conditions schoolchildren had to endure prior to the new building's opening in 1897, when the 'school' consisted of one room above the local shop. A total of 54 pupils crammed into the room during that school year and it must have been with some relief that the move was made to the spacious new premises.

Education became compulsory on Gigha in 1873 as School Boards were set up throughout Scotland – the result of government legislation. Among other things, the head teacher was responsible for keeping a log book – a duty which has been maintained to the present day. The head also had to collect the pupils' fees, a practice which was discontinued in 1890, when education became free.

The early entries in the first log book, – in immaculate copper-plate handwriting – contain numerous spelling and grammatical errors, which would suggest that the teacher had little in the way of formal training. Indeed, several inspector's reports written in the book draw attention to this. An inspector's visit to the school in the 1880's resulted in the suspension of a teacher for ineptitude shown. This teacher apparently merely asked pupils questions directly from a book and did not impart any knowledge to the class.

Matters improved, though, and the standards set in the Gigha school have enabled many pupils over the years to make their mark in higher education and the outside world.

The school log of bygone days refers frequently to absenteeism through inclement weather and sickness, with sore throats and colds being most common. The older boys invariably took unofficial holidays at potato lifting and harvest times.

In 1897, the school's annual holiday ran from August 2 until September 20, a total of seven weeks. There was no Christmas holiday that year but pupils were given one day off – December 31 – to celebrate Hogmanay. However, two years later, the log of December 28, 1899, reads: "Monday (Xmas) was observed as a holiday and the children were entertained on the evening of that day to a Xmas Tree etc through the kindness of Mr Scarlett."

January 5: "On Monday and Tuesday of this week school was closed – New Year holidays."

Come 1907, though, the yuletide break as we know it was introduced and the log states on December 24: "School closed today at one o'clock for New Year holidays. Re-opens January 6."

An enforced closure of the school occurred between July 2 and September 1, 1909 – the result of an outbreak of scarlet fever.

June 30, 1909: " The school was closed today on account of a suspected case of scarlet fever in one of the family of the headmaster."

July 2, 1909: "School closed by order of the Medical Officer of Health for the District."

In common with all rural and island schools the attendance roll on Gigha has steadily declined since the heady days of an 80-pupil school. Curiously, in 1978, there was something of a resurgence when 34 pupils were registered. Seven short years later the roll stood at just nine.

1897 - 54	1960 - 21	1995 - 09
1900 - 73	1973 - 24	1998 - 09
1914 - 58	1978 - 34	1999 - 08
1933 - 37	1981 - 22	
1945 - 24	1985 - 09	

There are presently 11 children under school age on Gigha and with the proposed re-opening of the landsite fish farm, it is possible that the roll will increase further.

The present head teacher, Mrs Lorna MacAlister, has been

on the island since 1981 and lives with husband Archie and son Neil in the schoolhouse sited alongside the main building.

Special correspondence courses, run from the former Argyll County Council education department in Dunoon, were formerly available to pupils who preferred to finish their education on Gigha, rather than attend secondary school in Campbeltown or Oban. The last pupil to complete such a course was, strangley enough, Mrs MacAlister's husband, Archie, in 1970, though Malcolm 'Malky' McNeill, of High Row, was actually midway through his course a year or two later when the practice was discontinued. Malky, now a fish farm worker with Gigha Fish Farms, was forced to attend Campbeltown Grammar School for the remainder of his schooldays.

Oban High School has a special hostel for island pupils but most Gigha children prefer to lodge with families in Campbeltown, thus enabling them to get home every weekend.

A gala day each year on Gigha is the school's open day and sale of work, an event which is extremely well supported by both islanders and visitors. The generosity of patrons enables Mrs MacAlister to take the children on various mainland excursions, including an annual visit to Glasgow during the Christmas pantomime season.

Cheese Galore

Wander along the dairy produce aisles in superstores with famous names such as Tesco, British Home Stores or Sainsbury and there is every chance that you will discover a goat's milk cheese on display which had its origins on Gigha.

The Inverloch Cheese Company, based at Leim Farm, on the southern end of the island, was formed eight years ago when the Eaton family moved from the Borders to Gigha. Headed by David senior, the Eatons formerly reared and milked goats in the Beattock area. However, the owner of their tenanted farm decided to sell up when heavy construction work involved in the upgrading of the A74 to motorway status caused all sorts of mess and upheaval. Added to this, the firm which the Eatons supplied with goat's milk decided to run down such operations so it was decided to inuagurate a cheese-making concern.

The tenancy of Leim Farm was available at this time and the Eatons successfully bid to become its new occupiers.

Previous cheese production on Gigha came to an unfortunate end nearly 20 years ago when the creamery at Achamore Farm was closed down following the discovery of a mysterious strain of bacteria in the water supply, resulting in the appearance of a type of fungus on the interior walls and ceiling of the premises. Eradication costs proved prohibitive and the decision to close down was made, which was a great pity as the Gigha Dunlop cheese was quite famous, being revered by connoisseurs far and wide.

However, the Inverloch Cheese Company has certainly put the island back on the map since it began marketing its creamy and uniquely flavoured cheeses.

A total of 300 goats and 15 Guernsey cattle are milked daily at Leim, which is run by David Eaton junior and his wife, Grace. The milk is expertly turned into cheese – goat's one day, Guernsey the next – by Miss Sheila McNeill, of The Croft. Sheila has been making the cheese at Leim for several years now and also keeps a few goats of her own.

The peak daily goat milk yield of approximately 70 gallons means a cheese production of about 150lbs every two days, though there is a two-month period when the animals do not milk. During this time, the cows' milk is used to make a thrice-weekly batch.

When the actual cheese-making is completed on Gigha, the raw material is transported to Campbeltown, where it is processed by a workforce of 12 at the Kirk Street premises of a former dairy. The move to the town was necessitated by the growing demand for the product and the shortage of workers on Gigha. The Campbeltown side of the business is directed by David senior and his wife, Kay. It is here that a wide variety of flavours are folded in to the cheese before waxing begins.

Particularly sought-after are the differently shaped waxed Guernsey milk cheeses such as apple, pear and peach, to which the respective fruit flavours are added. Other popular flavours include whisky, pickle, mustard, garlic, various herbs and a smoked version.

The cheese is marketed all over Scotland, England and the continent by English merchants. It does not come cheap, with a wholesale value of somewhere in the order of £5000 per ton. It has also found its way to the United States of America, Canada, Japan and Russia.

David Eaton junior, speaking of the success of the cheese, told me when I asked him why he thought it was so popular: "Well, we've got a great range. There is always one that someone is interested in."

The Guernsey dairy cattle's milk is also used to make Drumloch, the Eaton's brand name for a delightful cross between Cheddar and Dunlop which is in a class of its own.

Kay Eaton has always maintained that Guernsey cows are a superior breed when it comes to the quality of the milk required for making first class cheese. Having just sampled some, I concur, though I would respectfully suggest that, by the very nature of its lushness, the green grass of God's Island has something to do with it also.

Miscellanea

GIGHA has an amazing number of wells and natural springs. The water supply from such sources is ice-cold and has a tremendous quality. Arguably the purest water which can be drunk on the island comes from Tobar na Cloiche – well of the stones – on the west side.

Many a visitor has been grateful on a hot summer's day to Neil Bannatyne up at Cairnvickoye, who has erected a signpost advising of 'his' spring's presence and has even provided a drinking mug.

Several islanders actually prefer to use well water for domestic purposes rather than the mains supply.

It was at the source of the mains supply, a lochan known as The Dam, that an incident which could have had tragic consequences occurred many years ago. During an unusually cold spell, when the island was experiencing sub-zero temperatures, two estate workers, William McSporran and Angus Allan, decided to take a short cut across the frozen solid dam en route to Ardailly. The ice was inches thick but, unknown to them, a natural spring fed the lochan and when they neared its position the ice thinned alarmingly and cracked underfoot. Only a speedy reaction by the two men in regaining thick ice saved their lives. The constant movement of the spring water bubbling upwards had prevented thick ice forming and it was merely flake thick on the surface

THE distilling of illegal whisky, utilising any good quality excess barley, was a thriving cottage industry on Gigha right up until the end of the last century. Legally, there was one official distiller on the island who operated under the auspices of the proprietor.

However, apparently tales are still told today of many other 'aqua vitae' makers. The last known illegal still on Gigha produced whisky in the very house I sit in as I write, North Ardminish, which was a tenanted farm until five years ago.

The islanders had a cunningly effective early alarm system to warn of approaching officialdom. When any 'unwelcome' visitor boarded the small ferry at Tayinloan the boatman would hoist a different coloured sail to alert the populace.

Indeed, when excisemen made an unannounced call at Gigha in the 1890's, much whisky-making equipment was thrown into Tar an Tarb – Loch of the Bull – and one of the men involved fled to Glasgow, never to be seen on the island again.

MY FRIEND, James 'Jimmocks' McNeill, not long before his death showed me an interesting carving of a ship done on a stone in one of the fields of Ardlamy, near the old village settlement of Ardachy.

A young herd by the name of MacCallum was desperate to get to sea but domestic circumstances prevented this happening and he was required to work the land. Whilst engaged in his daily chores he saw a majestic schooner-rigged vessel passing Gigha on its way to some far-off port and he chiselled out an exact likeness of the sailing ship on a flat stone, which can still be seen today.

Some time later, the youth's seagoing aspirations overwhelmed him and, in the true romantic tradition, he ran away to join a ship. His story ended tragically, however, when he lost his life in a shipwreck off the Orkney Islands.

APPARENTLY there is a treasure trove hidden somewhere on Gigha. Three years' rent was secreted by the factor of the day due to a period of lawlessness and political unrest which affected the island for a while. The factor, however, died and nobody could find the hoard for years until it was discovered by a man called Stevenson, of Ardlamy, who shared it with his brother and housekeeper. But within days of his good fortune, the navy's infamous press gang descended on Gigha and Stevenson, having been warned, gathered all the cash together and hid it once more.

After serving in the navy for a number of years Stevenson became master of his own ship and sailed as a pirate. He ordered the crew of one captured ship to walk the plank and, as they were doing so, he heard one man sorrowfully announce that he would never see the Bull of Crero again. The Bull of Crero is a rock shaped like a bull's head on the islet of that name off Gigha's west shore. When Stevenson asked the man in which direction the animal looked he replied instantly: "To the north-east."

"You are right," answered Stevenson, and the man was immediately freed.

Stevenson, though, must have met with considerable success in his piracy venture for he never again returned to Gigha and the mystery of the money's whereabouts remains.

AS WITH most Scottish west coast islands, Gigha has had her fair share of shipwrecks over the years, ranging from small fishing craft to large ocean going vessels.

The last major stranding on Gigha was the Russian fish factory ship 'Kartli', which drove ashore on the west side a few days before Christmas, 1991. The 'Kartli' was damaged by a massive wave in horrendous storm conditions south-west of Islay. Four members of her crew were killed by the force of the sea which struck her bridge. The remaining crew members were rescued by helicopter and the disabled vessel, with 400 tonnes of frozen mackerel fillets on board, wallowed helplessly in the troughs of huge waves generated by gale force south-west winds.

Protracted salvage negotiations broke down and the ship, drifting on a north-easterly course, grounded at Port Ban, Gigha.

A number of cats aboard the 'Kartli' were rescued by the RSPCA and the frozen fish cargo treated with powerful chemical dispersants, though much of the surrounding coastline was scarred with assorted debris for a long time.

All that can be seen of the 'Kartli' above water now is part of her gantry-type masts.

ON BAGH Doirlinne (Isthmus Bay) opposite the northernmost point of Eilean Garbh (Rough Island), well protected from the elements in a niche of the cliff, is an interesting cave which was used by fishermen visiting Gigha from Kintyre at various times of the year, though it was finally abandoned early this century.

Six feet wide at its mouth, the cave is 25 feet high and 20 feet long. The fishermen, as well as using the cave as a base in which to repair damaged lobster gear, lived here when taking part in the Gigha fishery. Traces of ancient lobster pots can still be seen and many fishermen's initials, the earliest dating from 1735, have been cut into the sides of the cave. Parts of an old wall across the entrance still remain along with a flat stone slabbed walkway.

The Old Statistical Account (1793), in its reference to Gigha, mentions another prominent natural cave feature. It says: 'At the south end of the island, there is a subterraneous passage, 133 feet long, into which the sea runs. About the middle, there is an aperture eight feet long and two broad. Near the end there is another, 20 feet long and four broad. Round this aperture there are large pieces of rock; one of which has fallen in, and being jammed between the sides, divides it in two, and forms a convenient resting place for taking a depth of the chasm, which is here 22 feet, in the middle 32, and at the mouth 40. In a time of a westerly storm, being exposed to the great swells of the Atlantic Ocean, the sea rushes in with such violence as to discharge itself through these openings with thunderous noise, rising to an immense height, in the form of intermitting jets. Hence its name, Sloc an Leim, or squirting cave, literally jumping pit.'

Nothing has changed since the Account was written for I have witnessed the spectacle twice since coming to Gigha and it is, indeed, awesome.

THE REV William Fraser's Statistical Account of the Parish of Gigha written in 1791 for the General Assembly of the Church of Scotland tells us that the island's population was in excess of 600 and, despite what one may think, most people did not live on farms or off agriculture.

Apart from fishermen and farmers, Gigha supported weavers, tailors, shoemakers, general merchants, blacksmiths, millers and flax and kelp harvesters. There were boatbuilders, too, hard at work providing the many small boats owned on the island. Rev Fraser states that almost every family on Gigha possessed a boat either to cross to the mainland when conditions allowed or to fish the rich stocks of haddock, lythe, skate, mackerel and dogfish.

The blacksmiths were kept busy making all the iron goods

needed on Gigha. Examples quoted are pails, pots, cooking swees, anchors, chain and all kinds of farm implements.

Kelp harvesters enjoyed an excellent business relationship with a Dumbarton glass company. The seaweed was burnt in a kiln and the drawn off alkaline used, along with many tons of Gigha's silver sand, in the glass making process.

It has been suggested that the Drumeonbeg Crofts could have been kelp workers' dwellings and that Achnaha (Field of the Kiln) at the ferry catwalk may have been so named becuse it was there that the crop was processed.

AMONG the many relics left by Stone Age man on Gigha is a curious pair of standing stones named the Bodach and Cailleach – Old Man and Old Woman – which stand on a hillock near The Lodge. Islanders believe them to be very ancient and some people regard them with reverence, others with superstition. Standing only a few feet high, one stone is straight, while the other resembles a boat. Local lore decrees that should the stones fall over they must immediately be righted or the consequences will be serious.

Itinerant Irish potato dealers, who traded on Gigha as late as 1900, regarded the stones with the deepest of respect.

It is possible that the stones are of great antiquity since nobody yet has put a date on them.

IN 1942, a roof restoration programme affecting the houses at Ardminish prompted the arrival of outside labour, including a 70-year-old slater from Islay, a man whom I shall refer to as MacDiarmid. This man was a dedicated worshipper of his native isle's major export, whisky, but the amber nectar was in dreadfully short supply during the dark and austere days of wartime.

However, it was noted by some of Gigha's more attentive residents that MacDiarmid was often to be seen in a state of great jollity. This led to the general opinion that his merriment was brought on by the consumption of methylated spirits, a liquid much favoured universally by unfortunate individuals who had succumbed to the seduction of alcohol.

MacDiarmid was lodging with a Gigha man called Bob McMillan, who happened to be one of a number of men congregated in Angus McNeill's village shop of an afternoon. Another man, Angus Allan, asked McMillan: "Is it true that MacDiarmid is drinkin' meths?"

Bob's answer caused much laughter: "Well,it's like this. If ye stuck a wick in his backside an' lit it he would make a hell o' a good lantern."

THE SMITH brothers, Neil, Donald and Calum, who have been mentioned elsewhere in this book, shared the croft house at Drumeonbeg with their sister, who attended to the domestic duties of cooking, washing, cleaning and so on. They enjoyed a harmonious existence in the small house but all four agreed that an extra bedroom would be a most welcome addition to the building. At the earliest opportunity, the matter was drawn to the attention of the island factor but he, however, decided there was no real need for the construction of an extension.

He told them: "There is nothing wrong with the house at all. It will do the four of you fine; it's a right handy wee cottage."

Neil's reply has been recounted on Gigha many times and his comment to the factor was: "There's only wan thing it's handy for an that's at the New Year when we can all shake hands withoot gettin oot o' bed."

Calum, too, was always ready with a quick and witty reply and I recall another little gem he was responsible for. He was standing outside the Gigha shop and post office on a gorgeous summer's day, engaged in conversation with the proprietor of the time, Archie Wilkieson, when a day visitor asked to be directed to the best place for " a spot of recreation."

The shop is in the middle of the baseline of an imaginary triangle comprising the church, school, and hotel, and Calum replied instantly: "To your left is education, to your right is salvation and in front of you is damnation. What more could you ask for?"

IN THE days of not so very long ago, when all the Gigha farms had milk collected daily for cheese-making at the island creamery, local man Neil Bannatyne owned and drove the road tanker necessary for the operation.

In the interests of hygiene, the tanker had to be washed out each day and Neil sometimes refilled the lorry with fresh water to supply the needs of the many prawn and scallop fishing boats which used Gigha as a base each night. He was often given fish by the trawlermen in return for this service.

At that time, there was no fresh water hose at the South Pier as there is now and the Clyde Cruising Club's sailing directions advised yachtsmen that, among the other facilities available on Gigha: "Water can be had at the well." The spring in question is a good walk from the pier.

One evening, Neil spied a couple of nice haddock lying in a basket aboard one of the visiting vessels and he asked the skipper if he might have them, only to have his request denied out of hand by the tight-fisted fisherman.

Half an hour later, Neil was filling another boat's tank when he was approached by the same skipper, whose cook had informed him that their water supply was dangerously low.

When he asked that the tanker's hose be slotted into a filler on his boat, the skipper was stunned by Neil's speedy reply which has become folklore on Gigha: "Water can be had at the well!"

AN OLD Gigha man was sitting on a summer seat in the village, quietly enjoying a smoke of his pipe while appreciating the serenity of a glorious July afternoon. He was approached by an English tourist, who was perspiring copiously under a Harris tweed suit, waistcoat, plus fours and deerstalker hat.

Said the tourist: "I wonder at you, sir, sitting there. Don't you ever wish you could go to the mainland to see the sights?"

The islander looked the visitor up and down, slowly withdrew the pipe from his mouth and replied: "Now what would I be wanting to do that for when the sights come here to me!"

A SERMON delivered by the Rev Herbert Gunneberg in Gigha Parish Church which highlighted the horrific consequences of famine in Ethiopia troubled regular attender and elder John Martin deeply; so much so that he was determined to do something about it.

His philosophy that nobody in the UK, however needy, faces the ravages of starvation, spurred him to act and he decided to raise some money to alleviate at least some of the suffering.

Several fund-raising suggestions were rejected before John, the estate joiner, came up with a novel idea. He owns a heavily-built 16-feet-long clinker planked dinghy named 'Cille Chiaran' – the ancient name of the Royal Burgh of Campbeltown, of which John is a native – and he decided to do a sponsored 'row' by circumnavigating Gigha at the oars rather than by using engine power.

On August 12, 1995, John set off at 7.30am from Gallochoille on the first stage of the gruelling 16-mile journey and returned to the same spot at 2.30pm.

The trip was not without incident and John admits that he was pretty well all-in with a few miles still to go. However, sandwiches and a flask of hot, sweet tea that his daughter, Rhona, insisted he take with him provided the necessary sustenance to enable him to complete the course.

To make sure that the boat did not drift while he ate and rested, John made the 'Cille Chiaran' fast to a rock. To do this, he tied the light mooring line to his leg and jumped from the boat on to the reef. Replete after his break and a good smoke of his favourite pipe John found the last leg much easier to negotiate.

His efforts were well rewarded by various sponsors and the sum of £400 was forwarded to the Ethiopian Famine Appeal.

DURING the last week of August, 1997, yachtsman Frank Burns, a well-known visitor to the Ardminish Bay anchorage, sailed from Largs Marina round the Mull of Kintyre and dropped anchor at Gigha. Accompanying Frank on his trip north aboard the 'Kittiwake' was his partner, Rachel, and two dogs – a Jack Russell called Rosie and a Golden Retriever named Paddy.

The voyage seems to have been ill-fated from the start because shortly after arriving in Ardminish Bay a strong onshore breeze of east-south-east wind arose and they required the assistance of the local auxiliary coastguards to secure a more appropriate mooring. At this time, Rosie the Jack Russell disappeared and Frank and Rachel reckoned she had slipped over the side during the confusion.

The following day, Frank became unwell and boatman Kenny MacNeill had to ferry the island's district nurse, Margaret Wilkieson, out to the yacht to attend him. Margaret's advice to Frank to get on to dry land was heeded and it was decided to leave the boat at anchor, take the ferry to Kintyre the following morning and travel home to Taunton, Somerset.

Rachel was particularly upset at the disappearance of Rosie and, despite a thorough search of the 'Kittiwake' by themselves and the coastguard, no trace of the animal was found. She clung to the hope that Rosie had somehow managed to swim ashore and was safe on Gigha.

As the days wore on it appeared more and more likely that the dog had drowned and Rachel, in the belief that this was the case, bought another Jack Russell to replace Rosie.

Astonishingly, 14 days later, a yachstman aboard a sloop which had picked up the mooring next to the 'Kittiwake' heard a whimpering sound and investigations revealed a very much alive, albeit rather thin, Rosie.

Although it may appear to exceed the bounds of probability, the only way Rosie could have regained the 'Kittiwake' was by means of a bathing ladder slung over her stern. Frank and Rachel are adamant that the dog was not on board the 32-foot yacht when they departed, a view shared by the coastguard.

Several national newspapers showed an interest in the story and the matter was given considerable coverage.

GIGHA has, within the last few years, become a favourite listening post for a group of avid amateur radio hams from Glasgow, known curiously as The Windy Yetts Club. Its six male members formed the club 12 years ago and were issued with the call sign GM 4 VG.

They take part in an annual competition known as 'Islands on the Air', the aim being to contact as many islands as possible within 24-hours. Two years ago, The Windy Yetts were third in the world.

Technical and personal reasons endeared the lads to Gigha. Being surrounded by sea, contact with far-off places is made easier by the radio waves travelling over salt water rather than emitting from a built-up area, and the signal strength can be anything up to 1000 times greater. The equipment – seven 60-feet-high antennae – takes about 24 hours to assemble in the vicinity of the old ferry catwalk at Ardminish Bay. A mere two hours are all that are required to dismantle the gear.

The Windy Yetts returned to Gigha because of its friendly people and its natural beauty. Whilst on the island they renew acquaintances with Gigha's own radio ham, Ms Pat Monks, of Brae House. Pat, who is in her forties, is the proud holder of a Class A

Radio Amateur Certificate , awarded to her following a City and Guilds course and morse code test.

From her 'radio shack' on Gigha, she has conversed with other radio hams the world over, including Scotland, the United States of America, South America and Russia, using her comprehensive range of powerful sets.

A native of Blackburn, Lancashire, Pat moved to Gigha several years ago.

WINTER SABBATH ON THE ISLE OF GIGHA

It's November and the nights are drawing in
Yet the sky is still a blue so delicate,
Smudged with dabs of pure white cloud
As from a painter's palette,
Arching high and barely moving.

The stillness is so still
The copper of the dying bracken
Bright against the whin's dark green
Not even a soft call from birds
Disturbs the utter silence.

The Sound of Gigha drifts into the shore
Sundays allow this quiet peace
When for the day the strident ferry, tied up, rests
And Gigha, Gigalum and Cara merge mistily
In the timeless tide's oiled, reflecting glow.

VIE TULLOCH, 1995

A Look at the Past

As far as most schoolboys are concerned, history as an academic subject generally ranks fairly low in the popularity stakes. Indeed, as I recall, most of my Campbeltown Grammar School history periods were spent daydreaming about the efforts of a certain football team or the whereabouts of the local herring fishing fleet.

But a visit to Miss Betty MacNeill to talk about Gigha's past makes for compelling listening. Anyone crossing to the island seeking information about days gone by or family history are invariably told to "see Betty".

She lives with her brothers Malcolm and Kenny at Keill Cottage, a neat little house with panoramic views of Islay and the Atlantic Ocean. The presence of two 'pollags' – ancient corn grinding stones – beside the house give an indcation to her fondness for local history.

The day I called on Betty we sat in the cosy coal-fired kitchen at Keill as I listened to her lilting island voice describe the Gigha of old; the long gone village settlements, ancient burial sites, the productive wells of pure spring water and folklore tales.

There was a self-contained hamlet many, many years ago at Ardailly, on the west side of the island. Betty's description of the Ardailly village's proportions sounds so much more colourful than the clinical tabulation of house numbers and population: "If you stood at the mill in those days," she told me, "it would be possible to see the smoke rising from no less than 17 chimneys." A delightful description. There were also cottages at nearby Cairnvickoye and Tarbert Farm.

The ruins of the settlements are still just visible, as are the remains of another hamlet called Ardachy, also on the island's west side.

Betty remembers as a young girl during World War II joining her school classmates in Sphagnum moss gathering at Ardachy on Saturdays. The moss was used in the production of much-needed dressings for wounded servicemen. She has, of course, visited the site many times since and actually turned up a 1792 coin a few years ago with the aid of her metal detector.

Another fairly substantial cluster of cottages was situated at The Glen, an area of the hillside directly above the Gigha Hotel, though little evidence of this can be seen today.

One semi-ruin that Betty feels should be fully restored is the only surviving cottage of four at Carn na Faire, on Gigha's northern tip. There is an excellent well in the immediate vicinity and the last occupant of the house was one Sandy Orr, who doubled as a shoemaker and merchant.

Although Betty is avidly interested in the comparatively recent life and times of Gigha, she has an equally intense knowledge of the island's ancient history.

A mere two minutes walk from her home can be seen the evidence of an Irish presence of many centuries ago – the Oghan Stone. This stone, with barely recognisable script, is possibly the other part of another stone at the north end of the island. Betty told me that there are no fewer than 123 such stones in a southern Eire county and the Gigha carving was possibly done by Irish emigrants to remind them of their homeland.

Another interesting story concerns a grave sited just off the road at the left hand turn immediately past the cattle grid at Tarbert Farm. Apparently this grave contains the remains of an Egyptian woman who was drowned and washed ashore on Gigha hundreds of years ago. There are also mounds in the same area said to mark the graves of two monks who prayed there.

On a similar theme, Betty talked about the discovery of a 4000-year-old Bronze Age tomb at Kinererach Farm. This tomb was discovered by 17th century dyke builders who visited Gigha from the Borders area of Scotland. Six food vessels were in the tomb and the remains of a young female – much later established to be that of a 19-year-old – were found.

I also learned of the 5000-year-old chambered cairn burial site at Achamore Farm that Betty has walked past and wondered about for years. It was not until a lady visitor to Gigha from

London brought her attention to it and Betty confirmed through an official archaeological study that it was, indeed, an ancient burial ground.

Another small cemetery contains eight stone coffins. This is situated above a gully in the vicinity of the well-known 'twin sandy bays' on the north-eastern shore of Gigha. Human remains can be seen at this 4000-year-old site.

Betty has also in her possession a collection of artefacts which are of considerable interest. Included in her 'mini museum' is a fossilised sea urchin which is reckoned to be 20 million years old. She has also, in her lifetime, found vintage pieces as diverse as flint, quartz cutting implements, old glass bottle stoppers, coins, clay pipes, whisky bottles and a myriad of unique coloured stones.

She talks with enthusiasm of the stone gifted to her by farmer Kenny Robison, of Ardlamy. Kenny came across the $3^1/_2$ inch diameter flat circular stone in one of his fields. It has a perfectly shaped round hole in the middle and face markings. Betty has since discovered that it was part of a 3000-year-old primitive spinning aid.

One artefact that Betty would dearly love to see back on Gigha is a 16th century cannonball which was unearthed by the late Angus McNeill, as he ploughed his land at Kinererach Farm. Col James Horlick, the then laird of Gigha showed an interest in the find and borrowed it to have carbon-dating carried out in order to establish the cannonball's antiquity. Apparently it was taken off the island by a future proprietor and has never been returned.